Basic Principles and Practice of Business Administration

Basic Principles and Practice of Business Administration

DR. AMBROSE E. EDEBE,
MBA, PhD

Copyright © 2013 by Dr. Ambrose E. Edebe, MBA, PhD.

Library of Congress Control Number:	2013903717
ISBN: Hardcover	978-1-4836-0238-7
Softcover	978-1-4836-0237-0
Ebook	978-1-4836-0239-4

All rights reserved. No part of this book may be reproduced or transmitted in any form or by any means, electronic or mechanical, including photocopying, recording, or by any information storage and retrieval system, without permission in writing from the copyright owner.

This book was printed in the United States of America.

Rev. date: 03/14/2013

To order additional copies of this book, contact:
Xlibris Corporation
1-888-795-4274
www.Xlibris.com
Orders@Xlibris.com
129007

CONTENTS

Preface..9
Acknowledgements..11

PART ONE: PRINCIPLES OF MANAGEMENT 13

1. Introduction..13
2. The Nature of Management 13
3. Planning..14
4. Control 16
5. The Process of Control..16
6. Co-ordination 18
7. Motivation 18
9. Policy Formulation..19
10. Policy Implementation 20
11. The Framework of Management 21
12. Span of Control..23
13. Process of Delegation 24
14. Centralization and De-centralization......................................27
15. Leadership..28
16. Decision Making..29
17. The Social Responsibilities of Management...........................31
18. Committees..31
19. Channels of Communication 33
20. Reports and Report Writing 34
21. Form of Report 35
22. Management Techniques..35

PART TWO: THE HUMAN RESOURCE FUNCTION 38

1. Introduction..38
2. The Establishment 38
3. Recruitment and Interviewing..39

4. Training 39
5. Types of Training..40
6. Manpower planning 41
7. Job analysis..41
8. Promotion..42
9. Transfers..43
10. Withdrawals 43
11. Labor Turnover..43
12. Welfare..44
13. Safety and Health 45
14. Management by Objectives (MbO).................................45
15. Staff reports...46
16. Staff records 46
17. Wages and salaries Determination 46
18. Industrial Relations 47

PART THREE: THE PURCHASING AND MARKETING FUNCTIONS 48

1. The Purchasing Department 48
2. Purchasing Policy 48
3. Storage and stock Control 49
4. Marketing Functions Introduction 51
5. The 'Marketing Concept' 51
6. Marketing Policies...52
7. Market Planning 52
8. Market Research..53
9. Promotion...56
10. Advertizing..56
11. The Advertising Budget...57
12. Pricing and Costing...58
13. Public Relations 59
14. Distribution 59
15. Sales Management...62
16. The Sales Force 63
17. Sales Forecasting..64
18. Delivery 64
19. After Sales Service..64
20. Export Marketing..65
21. Product Development 66

PART FOUR: THE PRODUCTION FUNCTION 68

1. Introduction 68
2. Production Policy 68
3. Types of Production 70
4. Factory Location 72
5. Factory Layout 72
6. Estimating 72
7. Preliminary Planning 73
8. Production Planning and Control 74
9. Inspection 76
10. Materials Handling 77
11. Maintenance 77
12. Maintenance Control Department 78
13. Work Study 78
14. Value Analysis 80
15. Automation 81
16. Ergonomics 81
17. Research 81
18. Development 82
19. Design 83

PART FIVE: THE ADMINISTRATIVE FUNCTION 85

1. Introduction 85
2. Office Organization 85
3. Servicing Departments 86
4. Centralization of general services 86
5. Organization and Methods 87
6. Organization and Methods (O&M) in Operation 87
7. Charting 88
8. Mechanization 89
9. Limitations of mechanization 89
10. Electronic equipment 90
11. Computers 90
12. Methods of filing 90
13. Internal audit 91
14. Internal check 91
15. The Use of Forms 92

16. Design of Forms..92
17. The Use of Forms..92
18. Forms Control...93

Reference..95
About The Author...97

PREFACE

THE PRIMARY PURPOSE of this book is to provide students and others with a concise, thoroughly up-to-date book which will enable them to obtain a sound knowledge of the basic principles and practice of business administration for examination and practical purposes.

This book has been produced to make the learning of business administration simple as well as interesting, and intelligent study should equip the reader with a basic knowledge of business administration.

This book is a review and study guide. It helps in preparing for exams, in doing homework, and remains a handy reference source at all times. It will thus save hours of study and preparation time.

The book provides quick access to the important principles, definitions, strategies, and concepts in the field of business administration. Materials needed for exams can be reviewed in summary form—eliminating the need to read and re-read many pages of textbook and class notes.

ACKNOWLEDGEMENTS

I GIVE GLORY to God Almighty for making it possible for me to start and complete this book. May His name be praised!

I acknowledge the unflinching support received from my wife, Josephine, and the ceaseless prayers of my children—Sarah, Mary, Elizabeth, and Samuel—for my success. I would like to thank my father, Senior Apostle Thomas Edebe and my mother, Mother of Grace (Mrs.) Esther Edebe, for their unconditional love. I also wish to thank my brothers and sisters for their support.

Finally, I would like to acknowledge the support and contributions received from my professional colleagues. The book is all the better for their advice, but full responsibility for it rests with me.

PART ONE

PRINCIPLES OF MANAGEMENT

1. Introduction

THE STUDY OF management has increased substantially and the subject has been approached in many ways:

Three main classifications are:

a) The 'classical approach' (often termed 'Traditional Management') which studies technical activities, division of labor, specializations etc., and their co-ordination along the chain of command.
b) The 'human relations' approach which concentrates on the needs of the individual and views organizations from the point of view of group behavior. Emphasis is on employee participation and co-operation.
c) The 'systems approach' which views organizations from the point of view of a decision-making system. Concentration is on information needs of decision-makers and the design of communications channels. The actual task or function involved is viewed as subordinate to these. This 'approach' has currently come to the fore with the rapid advances of computer technology.

2. The Nature of Management

The activities of industrial undertakings can be divided into the following:

a) Technical (e.g. Production)
b) Financial (i.e. Provision and Utilization of Capital)
c) Commercial (e.g. Buying, Selling)

d) Accounting (i.e. Recording, Costing, Preparation of Accounts, Control Information)
e) Security (i.e. Protection of Property and Persons).

Management is a separate skill, though many persons who exercise a managerial function may have been trained in one or more of those techniques, e.g. a factory manager may be a qualified engineer, but when acting as manager he uses quite different skills and techniques from those understood as 'engineering'. The chief difference between the skill of management and the skill exercised in other crafts or callings is its human or social character; it is a responsibility exercised over other people, concerned with getting their co-operation and their unified response in the performance of a given task.

The following are broad classifications of the functions of management:

Planning: i.e. determining the broad lines for carrying out the operations (policy, general program, the overall plans, the organization) and planning the appropriate methods for effective action (equipment, tools, material supplies, working instructions, techniques, teams, etc.).

Control: i.e. checking current performance against predetermined standards, and recording the experience gained as a guide to future operations.

Co-ordination: i.e. balancing and keeping the team together by a suitable allocation of work among the members, and seeing that harmony is preserved among them.

Motivation (or ensuring morale): i.e. getting all members of the team to pull their weight effectively, to give their loyalty to the group so as to carry out properly the activities allocated to them and generally to play an effective part in the task undertaken.

3. *Planning*

The major difference between traditional and modern scientific approaches to management lies in the separation of planning from other aspects of management. As a specialized function, planning is akin to policy formulation. Where policy is concerned with future courses of action in general terms, plans provide detailed instructions to implement policy. Clear policy objectives are essential for successful planning.

There are two further prerequisites:

a) As plans are carried out in the context of a specific organizational framework, the organizational structure of the undertaking must be fully defined before plans can be drawn up.
b) Forecasts and predictions that the traditional manager based on guesswork of hunches are now calculated. Thus the provision of information needed for these calculations is crucial and must include all relevant factors, whether inside or outside the firm.

The weaknesses and limitations of planning are frequently due to lack of adequate information. Owing to this difficulty there is a tendency to confine planning to those activities that are predictable. However, if planning is to be comprehensive, suitable allowances must be made for the less predictable elements that may arise.

The main characteristic of a good plan is flexibility and no plan should be so rigid as to enforce conformity to the detriment of the exercise of initiative. Contingency allowances must be included to enable managers and supervisors to cope with the unexpected. Ideally the plan should set out a series of alternative courses of action together with information as to the probably outcome of each, from which management can choose.

Plans must outline activities within the scope of the resources available to the organization and be designed to guide those involved in the operations.

The aim of planning is to determine the requirements for attaining certain objectives. As a management tool it ensures unity of action amongst those carrying out the plans so as to achieve these objectives with the maximum economy in effort and resources.

4. Control

The control process falls into three parts:

a) setting standards of performance for a particular task.
b) checking how the task is currently performed, and
c) correction of deviations of current performance from planned performance.

Scientific control depends on measurability of the variable factors involved, enabling standards to be established. These can then be used to provide a basis for the evaluation of performance. The standards initially set are unlikely to be perfect but will undergo modification as managers become more experienced.

The link between the first and second parts of the process is the feedback to the controller of information so that any failure or deviation from the planned performance is immediately available together with reasons. Any necessary adjustments can then be made and the results of these corrections observed.

To be effective, control must be operated as a continuous process, otherwise deviation from planned performance may pass unnoticed or adjustments to rectify failures may be based on insufficient information and prove ineffective. Control becomes more complex as the size of organization increases. Delay in the feedback of information is more likely to arise and the information flow may be of such proportions that speedy decisions become difficult.

5. The Process of Control

The main task in the control process is the measurement of various parameters of the activity, and this may involve setting up staff departments whose responsibilities include collecting data as quickly and accurately as possible and supplying the data in the form of information which those controlling activities are then able to use to make decisions. Since control takes place following the preparation of plans, the ideal method of presenting information is to indicate where the actual results deviate from the plan, who is responsible and how serious is the deviation.

The seriousness of any deviation from a plan will depend, among other factors, on the calculation of the plan. Plans involving standards such as dimensions and quantities can be defined precisely. However, certain tolerances on dimensions may be permissible, and further, a degree of scrap may be regarded as inevitable. These matters must be dealt with at the planning stage so that deviations between actual and standard are regarded as avoidable. Nevertheless, it will still be important to bring the attention of management to deviations of significant nature, e.g. +/—5%.

Speed is a vital element in the provision of information to managers, and although the information is necessarily history when the manager receives it, it may still be presented in sufficient time for the manager to be able to avoid considerable loss of resources, where perhaps an adverse efficiency trend is occurring. The danger connected with late information is that it may provoke a manager to take action to solve a past problem which unfortunately aggravates a present one.

Those who initiate corrective action are the managers responsible for the activities. The staff personnel providing the information have no executive authority to give directions. It is worth emphasizing that the purpose of measurement is not to provide a stick with which to chastise the manager, but to aid him in the performance of his work. Those responsible for organizing the control procedures and the flow of documents must endeavor to build in a rapid feedback cycle for major variances from the target. For example, an excessive amount of scrapped work arising on a job ought to be brought to the attention of the manager before, or at the same time as, it is advised to those accumulating data about scrap. This will then ensure minimum delay in taking corrective action. The scrap report sent to the manager will then show the cost and quantity of all scrap arising in the week and provide an indication of the general level and trend of scrap in addition to the abnormal occurrences.

It would be unusual if a report, giving detailed figures of variance, indicated exactly what action was required by the manager. It is normally necessary for those issuing reports to explain the significance of the figures. This requires considerable skill and knowledge but it must be emphasized again that it is purely an advisory function.

6. Co-ordination

When a variety of tasks are to be performed by different types of people, each possessing different skills and capabilities, co-ordination is needed. Its importance is a feature of the growing complexity of modern business organizations.

Any enterprise consists of individuals, all of whom are capable of independent action. While their separate activities may be aimed at the same objective there is a danger that they may be working in different directions. The idea of co-ordination is to integrate individual efforts to produce a homogenous team.

To achieve this, all those taking part are kept informed on the activities of colleagues. Co-ordination is a process of continuous two-way communication. Managers should ensure full personal contact with subordinates. Effectiveness of any manager as a coordinator will be his attitude to his work and to other people as manifested in his personal relations.

The concern's organizational structure makes an important contribution to the task of co-ordination, provided it is well designed, defining staff responsibilities.

Management must ensure that co-ordination is implemented as a continuous procedure at the commencement of any activity and is maintained directly between the people involved. This element of personal contact links co-ordination to the other human element in the management process: motivation. This is especially relevant for the highest levels of management as co-ordination is not only integration of activities of immediate subordinates but also the ensuring that co-ordination is transmitted to lower levels of the organization.

7. Motivation

This involves directing people as a group towards some given aim and is partly a question of management leadership. The aim is to inspire people to direct their efforts to a common purpose so as to induce high morale. Motivation has two aspects:

a) the question of individual incentive, and
b) the individual's contribution to the integrated team effort.

In practice, motivation and co-ordination are parts of a dual process. This fits in with the functions of management which consist of blending the various human capabilities into a working team while preserving the strength of personal individualities.

Motivation is primarily a social skill. Management must be human as well as systemic and the influence of the emotional element of human make-up on people's behavior must be recognized. Thus, success in this aspect of management will depend not only on the innate ability and aptitude of the would-be manager but also on his readiness to recognize the specialist human character of the executive process and the need to be fitted for it by correct training.

9. *Policy Formulation*

The importance of 'policy' lies in providing management with a view of the intentions of the Board of Directors concerning the affairs of the enterprise and provides a basis for day to day decisions. A clearly defined objective for the concern is most important.

Policy formulation is the Board of Directors' responsibility and is a corporate responsibility rather than that of any individual Director. Major formulation takes place during Board meetings, usually in the context of some specific decision. Modifications of policy in detail occur frequently due to changes in circumstances surrounding the concern's operations.

It is important that senior managers are aware both of company policy and their own responsibilities, so that their decisions are not radical departures from the Board's wishes.

Policy formulations must consist of two types of statements:

a) General policy, consisting of statements of objectives and general principles which constitute a set of standards governing company operations. These are an aid to management in routine decisions which deal with the standards of conduct to be observed in the

relations between the enterprise and (i) the community and (ii) the employees.
b) Sectional policy, designed to give detailed instructions to various sections of the organization.

In a well-managed concern there are series of inter-related processes all hinging on the idea of policy:

a) collection and examination of information to provide a framework for policy decisions;
b) interpretation of the formulated policy into instructions to management;
c) communicating policy and instructions to relevant personnel;
d) the application of policy by management by translating it into plans;
e) checking on the implementation of these plans by means of controls;
f) reviewing existing policy in the light of changing circumstances leading to modifications and departures from the original formulations.

The ideal policy should be flexible to allow for changing circumstances, but at the same time would conform to the need for continuity in order to provide management with a stable framework within which to operate.

10. Policy Implementation

To make full contribution to the success of an enterprise, management decisions must be based on clear policy directives setting out the general characteristics of the activities to be pursued to achieve the concern's objectives.

Just as the formulation of policy is the responsibility of the Board of Directors, its actual implementation is the task of management. The major prerequisite of an effective policy is that it should be capable of implementation in terms of the resources of plant, labor and finance available. There must be a 'channel' through which the Board can ask management for comments and advice prior to making its final decision. This procedure guarantees the practicability of the resulting policy directives and constitutes a powerful contribution to executive morale by providing a sense of participation in company affairs. Communication between management and Board keeps the latter informed of the progress of the enterprise and provides a check that policy is implemented along the predetermined lines. The 'channel' is the Managing Director or the Chief Executive.

Policy directives will provide the broad courses of action that the Board would like each section to pursue. The executive heads of each section must interpret the relevant parts of these directives and determine the required action. The various sectional policies are interlinked and while this may have been allowed for, in theory, at Board level, overall co-ordination is needed to ensure that this applies in practice. Responsibility belongs to the Chief Executive and can be discharged at regular meetings of section heads, where each participant contributes his own interpretation of the Board's overall policy and assists in the integration of the various sectional policies from a practical point of view.

If the purpose of policy is to enable the full range of activities of the concern to be more easily coordinated, it is necessary that all important decisions be taken in the light of relevant aspects of the Board's directives. To avoid excessive referring back along the line of command it is vital that the information on company policy is available at all levels so that appropriate decisions may be taken.

There are limitations that need to be observed in the communication of policy information. To inform people fully of aspects of policy which do not affect them directly may encourage confusion rather than co-ordination, while every company has certain areas of policy which need to be kept, if possible, from competitors.

11. The Framework of Management

An important responsibility of management is the design and maintenance of an organization structure. This provides a framework within which the process of executive control can exist. It also provides part of the mechanism for discharging management responsibilities. An organization structure consists of a scheme of responsibilities attached to particular positions, or particular individuals, and of the formal relationships existing between various executives in the performance of their duties.

As a management tool, an organizational structure is concerned with planning and coordination, its chief purpose being to ensure the smooth and balanced working of the enterprise. It is able to do this by removing any potential misunderstanding as to which particular individuals. As the preparation of a scheme necessitates a review of the particular tasks undertaken by management, a clearer understanding can be obtained of the nature of the various tasks and of the number and type of relationships that should exist between specific executives. The design of an effective organizational structure automatically involves the setting up of effective coordination machinery.

The key to this framework of management is a 'schedule of executive responsibilities' setting out the responsibilities of the various managers and the formal relationships to their superiors and subordinates. If this document is prepared in a pictorial manner it becomes the familiar organizational chart, but without these schedules the chart provides only a partial view of the position.

Organizations vary in structure, according to the nature of the concerns activities. The commonest structure has a Managing Director answerable to a Board of Directors and having as subordinates, managers responsible for various operational activities. These **line** executives are **functional** executives who provide specialized services and act in an advisory capacity to the line executives. Whether or not they are separately embodied in the person of individual executives, all organizations must contain both functional and line elements. The formal relations that exist between individual executives are:

a) Those between a senior and his subordinates. Such direct or 'line' relations are basically those of giving instructions and carrying them out.
b) Those between the specialist functional executive and the line manager and subordinates. Although the specialist is responsible to top management for the supply of a particular service he has no direct authority over the people using it, who come under a Line Manager. Such relations are indirect or functional.

c) Relations will exist between the staff officer, or personal assistant, to a manager and to other personnel. An assistant has no authority and involve the relations of the Manager to whom he is attached. These are 'staff relations'.
d) Individual executives have specific responsibilities. The fulfillment of a specific role involves collaboration with colleagues having related areas of responsibility. There exists a relation between executives working in parallel sections who are either responsible to the same superior or to superiors of comparable status. These are 'lateral relations' and depend largely on co-operation at an informal level.

12. Span of Control

The limitation of human ability and time make it necessary to divide an organization into areas of responsibility under the control of a manager. The number of immediate subordinates whose activities the manager is expected to supervise is known as the Span of Control, and has to be determined at all levels of management.

The span of a manager's control should not be increased to the point where his subordinates are denied ready access to him and so experience frustration. Furthermore, if the span is too wide it will force managers to delegate responsibility to such an extent that adequate supervision becomes difficult. On the other hand, if the span is too limited little delegation will result which may in turn discourage subordinates from using their initiative.

It is often difficult to determine the optimum span of control, but the following factors need to be considered when reaching a decision:

i) **The nature of the work done**
If the subordinates have specific uniform jobs which do not interlock, the numbers can be relatively large. However, where jobs interlock and decisions affect the work of others, the number of possible relationships and hence the complexity is governed by the numbers involved, often causing the span of control to be narrower.

ii) **The quality of the superior and the subordinates**

This involves mental capacity, knowledge, experience, interpersonal skills and relationships.
iii) **The cohesiveness of the subordinate group**
If a group of subordinates are accustomed to working as a team much of the strain of supervision will be removed from the manager responsible and so enable the span of control to be extended.

Increased mechanization and availability of management services have tended to reduce supervisory requirements, thereby increasing the span of control.

13. Process of Delegation

Administrative organizations by their very nature create executive / subordinate relationship and it is vital that these relationships are wisely defined and clearly understood.

In the process of delegation certain major issues arise, e.g.:

a) What happens to authority and responsibility in the process of delegation?
b) How can the ideas of staff and functional authority be used to advantage?
c) Under what conditions is decentralization desirable?

It is necessary to understand what is meant by the various terms of authority which are often confused, i.e.:

Legal Authority

When an individual is permitted to take an action, e.g. the Purchasing Manager placing a contract this is known as legal authority, although this authority is not usually of particular concern in the administrative process.

Technical Authority

This stems from an individual being recognized as an expert in some particular field. Advice from such a person is sought not because of the position he holds but because of the personal knowledge he has on a particular issue. Technical authority adheres to the individual and it cannot be assigned. An executive will frequently possess legal (or administrative) and technical authority.

Ultimate Authority

This is concerned with the original source from which the right to take a certain action is derived. In modern times, society as a whole expects businesses and governmental departments to perform definite services and has granted at least minimum authority for the executives of these enterprises to carry out their respective tasks.

Operating Authority

Delegation of authority at the operational level can be stated as giving someone permission to do certain things. Assuming the executive making the delegation is himself authorized to take such action he merely extends the permission to subordinates, usually indicating how such permission is to be used.

Delegation may consist of simple delegation which usually involves superiors delegating repetitive tasks and a minimum amount of associated planning to a single subordinate.

In larger organizations, delegation may be to several subordinates, who in turn may undertake further delegation. In carrying out this more complicated procedure, decisions such as how the work is to be appointed and how much planning should be delegated, are two vital issues which have to be decided.

There is a real need for the limits of authority to be clearly understood. This may be by way of the implication of general limits, i.e., that action should be in accordance with company policies, procedures and programs. Alternatively, specific limits may be spelled out with regard to each executive.

Although the basic idea on delegation appears relatively simple, in addition to the need for recognizing and defining the limits on authority, the following points must be borne in mind.

i) *Responsibility cannot be delegated*
Even when an executive has delegated a duty to a subordinate he is still responsible for its proper performance, although it may be necessary in practice to give some recognition to the operating situation. When delegation and re-delegation is necessary to accomplish a large task, the possibility of human error increases but this may be seen to be more a matter of standards of performance than one of responsibility. Delegation will not have removed the accountability, but appraisal may be tempered somewhat by the extent to which an executive must rely on subordinates to carry out the work.

ii) *Dual subordination must be avoided*
A person cannot serve two masters, he should have one line supervisor otherwise confusion and frustration will result. For the same reason, by-passing the normal line relationships should be avoided although there are certain cases when it is beneficial but they should be restricted to exchanging information and ideas, and not for giving directions. Bypassing is also permissible in a typical grievous procedure to enable an employee to carry a complaint over the head of his immediate superior in the event of a dispute.

iii) *Authority should equal responsibility*
If an employee is given considerable scope of action he should be held accountable for the outcome. On the other hand he cannot be held accountable for results that he is not permitted to guide according to his own best judgment. In many cases authority is diluted by circumstances outside the person's control (the Sales Manager does not have the power to make customers buy if they find competitors' products more attractive). Strictly speaking, in such cases, responsibility is correspondingly reduced and this is widely recognized in practice. Very often a person is expected to have a feeling of responsibility that far exceeds any authority

he has been granted and such a concept involves a moral concern beyond the immediate scope of the individual, implying he can be held accountable for sensing potential trouble and attempting to get it corrected.

14. *Centralization and De-centralization*

Neither absolute centralization nor absolute de-centralization is practicable, major issue having to be decided by the central authority whilst day-to-day decisions are made at the various managerial tiers.

The extent to which centralization or de-centralization takes place will be decided by numerous factors which may include the managerial style of the organization, the size of the understanding, the extent of diversification of the enterprise, the type of technology in which the company operates, the ability of middle and junior management, and the effectiveness of communications systems within the company.

In most organizations, a balance is achieved between centralization and de-centralization with all the major decisions being made by the central authority including the formation of the framework in which any de-centralization would operate.

Those who support a high degree of centralization would claim such advantages as better overall managerial control, standardization and increased economy and flexibility in the use of resources, whilst de-centralization may have the advantages of improving morale, avoiding frustration of middle and junior managers and the minimization of bureaucracy.

De-centralization may be hampered for a number of reasons. These include, in some instances, the reluctance to delegate which may stem from lack of confidence in subordinates, the lack of ability of executives to communicate to subordinates what is required, the absence of adequate controls to give warning of impeding problems. Furthermore, de-centralization may be difficult due to subordinates attempting to avoid responsibility for such reasons as preferring to rely on other people, the fear of criticisms for mistakes, the lack of necessary information and resources, an already full workload, lack of self-confidence and the inadequacies of any positive incentives.

15. Leadership

This is the ability to inspire others by personality and example. Basically, it means the manager's ability to choose the right subordinates to weld them into a team and to bring out in them the need for self-discipline. Leadership implies that the manager accepts responsibility for achievement of the group objective, but it also implies that he cannot achieve it alone and that he requires the co-operation of his team. The manager that can get a full response from his team owes his success at least partly to them. The Board of a company must see that its representatives combine authority with leadership.

It is usually true that no section, department or undertaking can be better than the man at the top. This is not so important when the work is largely routine and the manager is fortunate enough to have assistants who are conscientious as well as capable.

The importance of the individual is becoming more recognized. Before a person can be induced to behave in certain desirable ways, a knowledge of human psychology is needed. As an individual, each person thinks and reacts slightly differently from others in similar situations. He has certain qualities and feelings which make him an individual and he requires individual treatment if the right relationship is to be built up between himself and the manager.

True recognition of an individual involves knowing many facets of his nature. But in the work situation only one aspect of the person is seen. Hence the need for sympathetic observation and treatment to reduce the initial barriers between managers and subordinates. Unless the manager has a genuine regard for people and their feelings, their points of view and their potential, he will fail to convey a sense of respect.

Unless good human relationships exist, most schemes to increase productivity and to motivate people in a particular direction will fall short of their objectives. If employees are unhappy, suspicious and disgruntled there will be higher labor turnover, absenteeism, poor workmanship and lack of discipline.

A Management policy to improve human relationships must be a long-term one as such changes do not happen overnight—often the mere act of attempting to improve the situation is treated with doubt. Employees gradually begin to change their attitude towards work when they get opportunities to use their initiative and abilities to greater advantage.

16. Decision Making

It falls to the manager to make decisions during the course of every working day. There are various kinds of decisions, which may be summarized as follows:

a) Initial plans are formulated by senior management and communicated down the line to lower levels. Each manager decides the action required of his department or division in order to meet stated objectives.
b) In the execution of plans, employees may face unforeseen problems and will require their immediate manager to clarify past policy decisions or revise them. Also, deviations from plan may require corrective decisions to be taken.
c) Whereas the circumstances may be such that there is plenty of time in which to arrive at a decision, situations will inevitably occur where a crisis develops and there is very little time to obtain all the information necessary for a decision. The experience of the manager and an ability to comprehend facts rapidly will affect the quality of the decision made.

In arriving at a decision in any sphere, certain stages can be clearly seen:

a) The manager must have a clear understanding of the aims and objectives of the business which will provide the basis of all decisions.
b) The circumstances giving rise to a decision must be fully analyzed, and the maximum amount of relevant information obtained.

c) The information will probably suggest various alternative courses of action that could be taken, and the manager must compare these—the costs, likely outcomes and effects on other departments etc.—and come to a decision.

Various factors will affect the way in which a decision is made:

a) How urgent is the matter?
b) Has the manager the authority to give a decision?
c) What are the financial implications of the decision?
d) What information is available?
e) How long will it take to obtain additional information, and at what cost?

The more urgent the matter, the more important will it be to arrive at a correct decision quickly and not spend precious time debating who should make the decision. This will depend however, on the sums of money being committed, since it may be better to spend money as the result of delaying a decision so that vasts sums are not mis-spent.

A procedure manual can sometimes help in these situations, in that this kind of problem is thought out beforehand. That is to say, the manual should lay down very clearly the amount of expenditure for which particular levels of management may commit the company without reference to a more senior manager. The arrangements should be so designed that it is always possible to make contact with a manager who has sufficient authority.

Lack of information is often a hindrance in coming to a decision, but if the matter is relatively insignificant then even if the decision is wrong the results are not too serious. It is, of course, important for management to provide for itself an adequate information service in respect of speed, detail, and accuracy. It must be noted that old information may be very misleading and may cause bad decisions, because management may be seeking to cure a problem that does not now exist and so exacerbate current problems. Where masses of information are involved, the company must consider if it can afford not have fast data processing equipment and also access to specialists such as statisticians and operational research workers who are able to limit the area of uncertainty involved in the decision.

17. The Social Responsibilities of Management

Management must admit wider responsibilities than those contained in its constitution, i.e. than the mere provision of a service in the case of a nationalized body, or the making of profits in a private enterprise organization. These wider responsibilities include the following:

i) To the staff and work people—Conditions of employment should be such that each employee is fairly impartially treated, that opportunities for advancement exist and that reasonable security and conditions of work are provided. Frequently, payment during sickness is made and a pension scheme is provided. In larger firms social activities are arranged to help foster esprit de corps.

ii) To the Trade Unions—The duty of consultation with the unions at all levels is now generally admitted by management and those employees who are officials of a union are usually granted facilities to carry out their union duties.

iii) To other members of the industry—In most industries there is a Trade Association whose duties are to promote the interest of the industry vis-a-vis the Government and other industries, to negotiate with the Trade Unions at national or regional level and to carry out public relations work. Membership of such a Trade Association usually carries with it an obligation that the member will not act in any way which is detrimental to the industry as a whole.

iv) To customers—Fair standards of trading must be maintained.

v) To society—A responsibility to society devolves upon an undertaking because of its participation in the life of the community.

18. Committees

When formulating a committee, its terms of reference must be clearly understood by all concerned, not least of all its members. Many misunderstandings have occurred because bodies which were under the impression that they had executive powers found subsequnetly that their role was nothing more than advisory.

There are various forms of committees including:

i) **Managing**—which could be, for example, the Board of Directors who retain full executive responsibility.
ii) **Executive**—which usually consists of a number of senior managers. The purpose of this committee is to regulate the day-to-day operations of the organization.
iii) **Advisory**—A committee of this type is usually set up to consider and make recommendations on a specialist topic.
iv) **Co-ordinating**—In large complex industrial organizations, coordinating all the various activities is one of the most difficult tasks and the setting up of the various interests can go a long way to solving this problem.
v) **Conciliatory**—In the main these are established in an attempt to solve industrial disputes.

Many arguments are voiced for and against committees and the arguments to support the establishment of committees may be summarized as follows:

a) They provide a superior problem-solving procedure in that the problem may be more rationally considered by a number of people rather than an individual, and that it is unlikely that a number of persons would make the same error simultaneously.
b) A problem can be considered by segregating it into its various components for specialist consideration which should increase the speed at which decisions are reached.
c) Committees provide the platform for consultation and a democratic exchange of views which it may be claimed acts as a motivator for people, enabling them to contribute more fully and effectively.
d) Committees provide opportunities for greater numbers of people to participate in decision-making and problem-solving and also provide a means of communication between members of different subgroups which in turn may lead to increased cohesiveness within the organization.

e) Committees may provide excellent facilities for education and training thus enabling the members to play a more active role subsequently.

On the other hand, those who argue against committees would undoubtedly raise the following objections:

a) Their operations are costly, time consuming and inefficient, although possibly the worst effects could be overcome by the use of efficient procedures and the presence of an effective chairman.
b) Dominating personalities and minority interests can often be more influential over the committee proceedings than their relative numerical strength justifies.
c) A committee which consists of members of unequal rank may experience some psychological problems; for example, subordinates feeling unable to speak freely and consequently not making their fullest contribution.
d) Individual members of a committee may not feel personally accountable for any decision taken, claiming that they were only one of a number or that the decision was not unanimous.
e) For the sake of expediency, any decision reached may be nothing more than a compromise which may not be representative of any individual view.
f) Committee proceedings may be thwarted by an individual who insists of having his own way or by personal prejudices.

19. Channels of Communication

In a large organization, the volume of transactions is considerable and a number of specialized departments and sub-departments exist, each dealing with a single and perhaps narrow aspect of a course of action. It is essential to formalize the transmission of instructions and information so that everyone concerned is fully briefed. In a small organization, instructions and information need to be conveyed only to a few persons (or only to one) as the range of duties of each is usually wider. In such organizations, therefore, the need for formal channels of communcations is not so great, but in a large organization 'communcation' is an extremely important part of supervision and the channels or lines of communication must be carefully planned.

The channels of information for the passing down of instructions should follow the organization structure. Annoyance may result if a person possessed of responsibility is by-passed by sending the instructions direct to his subordinate. Emergencies may arise, however, when prompt action is necessary, and in such cases it may be desirable to give courtesy copy of the instructions to the person responsible, the actual instructions going direct to the subordinate whose duty it is to take the necessary action. The channels of communication should be under constant review by higher management to ensure that blockages do not occur.

Facilities must also exist for information to pass upward—e.g. data for management decisions; the putting forward of staff opinions.

20. Reports and Report Writing

Most supervisors find it necessary from time to time to give an account of some event or events to their superior officer. Such accounts are, for important matters, made in writing and termed 'reports'.

Reports should be written in clear simple English. Extravagant and sweeping statements should be avoided and any conclusions should be based on adequate evidence. The report should not be conversational in tone and its matter should be assembled and set out in a logical manner. For easy reading, adequate use of paragraphs and sub-headings should be made. It is usually preferable to include figure tabulations, plans, graphs or photographs in an appendix or appendices, each being clearly referenced to the appropriate paragraph of the report. If the paragraphs are numbered consecutively, reference from one to another is facilitated. The report should be as brief as possible, all matter which is not strictly essential being omitted, but if the report is necessarily long, an index should be included.

Though the writer should have made full investigation of the facts and circumstances germane to the subject to enable him to report in a balanced and unbiased manner, he should avoid confusing the reader with matters he deems irrelevant. Conclusions should be unambiguous.

21. Form of Report

Because of the variety of the subject matter, it is impossible to lay down a hard and fast form which the report should take. It may, however, include sections as follows:

a) The name(s) of the person(s) to whom the report is addressed and of the persons to whom copies are to be sent.
b) A brief heading indicating the subject-matter.
c) Introduction or terms of reference. This section should clearly set out the subject-matter, quoting the words of the person who called for the report or the minute of the committee requiring it.
d) The body of the report. This section should set out the inquiries made and any limitations thereon if the report is of an investigatory nature. If of an explanatory nature, this section will assemble all facts and opinions germane to the inquiry, giving sources and authorities.
e) The conclusion. This section should clearly set out the writer's opinion on the subject-matter, and should flow logically from the facts and opinions set out in section(d).
f) Recommendations. If the report is investigatory, and the conclusions drawn require implantation by executive action, a list of the writers' recommendations should be given.
g) Appendices. If these are numerous an index should be provided.

22. Management Techniques

Various techniques are available to help the manager, but it must be emphasized that they are merely tools. They are no substitute for management. The manager must still manage, using the technique as an aid but never ruled by it.

Senior management must exercise great care in introducing new techniques by not imposing them on unwilling managers but educating them by explaining their value. A technique such as budgetary control or work study which is not properly introduced and applied may destroy the harmonious working of a department and create more problems than it solves.

Some of the techniques applicable to specific aspects of business are discussed in those parts of the course dealing with separate departments. In addition, there are techniques relevant to management generally and some are summarized below.

a) **Automation.** A production process where the control is built into the system, i.e. the subsequent steps in operation are pre-set, and take place automatically without further intervention by an operator. Numerically controlled machines are a prime example, where instructions on each successive stage of the production process are encoded on a magnetic or punched tape, which then activates each progressive changeover in the process.

The four successive stages of automation are:

i) 'Open Loop' control—mostly conventional instrumentation, where an operator watches individual guages, compares them with instructions, then moves to controls and adjusts each one manually. 'Open Loop' means that control is not self-contained; the man must look, decide, and then act.
ii) 'Semi-Open Loop' control—the operator works in a central control room and operates a control panel which adjusts plant processes. Operations are mechanical, but final control is still in the hands of the man.
iii) 'Closed Loop' control—computer reads instruments and compares findings with pre-set instructions, automatically adjusting control to keep conditions steady. Operator only interferes if something goes obviously wrong.
iv) Fully automated control—instruments send messages to central computer which keeps processes lined up to correct level and adjusts them to optimum production. A 'fail-safe' control may be established whereby at any failure plant automatically shuts down and gives warning.

b) **Critical Path Analysis** (Network Analysis, PERT). A technique enabling the making of logical decisions by illuminating priorities in complex situations over time and spotlighting the shortest possible time in which a project can be completed.

It uses an arrow-diagram or 'network' to illustrate the interrelated sequences. The longest sub-sequence which determines the length of the total operation time is the Critical Path—all other sequences take less time, therefore resources can be switched, delayed or planned anew.

    c) **Operational Research (O.R.).** The application of scientific disciplines to the evaluation and planning of large-scale, complicated operations. O.R. usually proceeds by stages:

       i) Definiton of problem; fact-finding
       ii) Model-building—A 'model' is a simplified representation of reality (e.g. an organizational chart is a 'model'). This allows the isolation of crucial factors and the formulation of hypotheses about their relationships. (Does movement in one factor, say, sales, affect another factor, say costs?)
       iii) Quantification of the model, by applying values to each factor—based on available data or additional observation.
       iv) Validation: projecting the consequences of change in selected factors and comparing results with known facts (e.g. comparison of forecasts with actual performance).
       v) Application of results to real situations to bring them as close as possible to the optimum predicted by the model.

A number of recognized techniques have been developed such as linear programming, forecasting techniques, queuing theory. O.R usually applies mathematical language, and for most O.R. operations, in view of the immense number of calculations, computers are essential.

    d) **Simulation.** An application of O.R. model-building for the purpose of representation, investigation and experiment. By varying the input factors into the model, one can clarify the relative importance of these factors; one can see and assess the response to input variations and the importance of different outcomes to decisions. Varying outcomes can be predicted on a 'what happens if . . .' basis, without costly experiments in actuality.
    Its uses in inventory control, production, scheduling, warehouse planning etc. have proved very valuable.

PART TWO

THE HUMAN RESOURCE FUNCTION

1. Introduction

THE HUMAN CONSTITUENTS (i.e. men and women) of an organization receive an increasing amount of attention in modern times, partly due to the growth in size of business undertakings and greater needs for education and training. The influence of trade unions and the general development of ideas on human relations have also played a part.

All executives and supervisors have a general responsibility for maintaining good human relations so that the various members of the organization may be welded into a team. In a large business, it may be necessary to employ a human resource manager as a specialist in the field of personal relations. He is responsible for advising the managing director on the formulation of personnel policy, and planning and supervising the procedures by which that policy is carried into effect.

He also renders a service to other executives, by selecting and engaging employees, preparing records and returns, investigating the causes of absenteeism and providing canteen and medical facilities and other welfare services. Apart from his own staff he has no 'line' responsibilities or duties, but holds a functional responsibility for all personnel matters.

2. The Establishment

The human resource manager is responsible for the maintenance of the concern's total 'establishment'. The 'establishment' is found by working out the various tasks which have to be performed and relating these to the jobs performed by individual employees. To maintain the establishment, replacements should be organized to fill the vacancies that will be continually occurring. Ideally, this should be done on a planned basis, but in many cases staffing is governed more by obvious and immediate needs than by rational projections of manpower requirements.

3. Recruitment and Interviewing

When a vacancy occurs, the human resource officer will use the job profile to draft a suitable advertisement which will set out the essentials of the job, qualifications required, salary etc. It should then be circulated to the various sources of applicants, e.g. labor exchanges, professional registers, the press. Applicants are then analyzed and a questionnaire may be issued to selected applicants.

After evaluation of the completed questionnaires, short listed applicants are invited for interview.

At least two persons should interview applicants: the human resource officer, to assess the suitability of the candidate from the point of view of his personal characteristics, and the relevant line manager to evaluate the candidate's technical capabilities.

4. Training

This should be systematically organized and integrated into the company's manpower policy. Training thus becomes closely tied to manpower planning, selection and promotion.

The pace of industrial technology has entailed emphasis on the continuity of staff training at all levels because of the growing need for retraining and refresher courses. The need for training in human relations becomes increasingly important as work relationships become more complex.

The cost of training new employees in terms of spoiled work, slow production, lecture and training time, etc., is frequently considerable and if an employee leaves this expenditure is lost. Therefore, the suitability or otherwise of a new entrant for a particular job should be quickly ascertained.

5. *Types of Training*

   a) **Induction Training.** The purpose is to welcome the newcomer and generally to help overcome the personal difficulties of entering a new situation. It should be a planned exercise in the course of which the new employee becomes acquainted with the products, policies and problems of the concern and with the members of the organization. He will also be given information on his own position. Further training is always necessary. Semi-skilled job training usually takes only a few weeks. The trainee is gradually introduced to the actual work and, under supervision, encouraged to do it. Such training may be done 'on-the-job', i.e. in the workshop but is preferable to acquire the skills in a separate training room or establishment where the demands of the work process do not distract from learning and where initial mistakes can be corrected in a more suitable atmosphere.
   Job-training may be supplemented by day release to a local education institute, where, besides broadening the employee's skill, a greater background knowledge about both the job and the industry can be imparted.

   b) **Craft Training** usually relies on the apprenticeship system. Apprentices, as they progress, spend an increasing part of their time in actual production. The organization of their training usually involves a period of external training by day release and sandwich courses.

   c) **Training of Supervisors.** Foremen and other supervisory staff are the first line of management and, apart from particular skills, the performance of their tasks requires additional knowledge, e.g. the company's organization and policies, new production techniques and human relations.

   d) **Office Training** often takes prior skills (e.g. typing) for granted and concentrates on teaching correct administrative procedures, the handling of office machinery and the role of office work.

   e) **Management Training** ranges from the induction of graduates to symposia for managing directors. As the management field is currently an area of major innovation e.g. in marketing, operational research, corporate planning etc., there has been a corresponding increase in seminar conferences and similar training aids.

Management training can be viewed either as specialist training in a particular business function or as generalist training covering the knowledge, skills and techniques of management (e.g. organizing, planning, control etc.). The essential point is to enable its practitioners to learn an analytical approach to decision-making and to implement this through other people.

In the larger firms the training function is placed under a training officer who is responsible for the selection and supervision of trainees, planning courses and assessment of results.

6. *Manpower planning*

This is a form of budgeting in that it entails the forecasting of staffing requirements. The aim is to achieve a flow of labor which will provide the total work force in each category of labor at the time of need. Not only must new recruits be available to replace those leaving but also promotions must be planned on an overall survey. The planning must be a continuous process to include any future expansion of the firm and any areas where new types of skills will be required.

7. *Job analysis*

Job analysis aims at setting out in a systematic manner the conditions of a particular job. The line manager contributes a statement of the technical requirements of the job which includes the sequence of activities involved.

The human resource manager will assess the human requirements, e.g. the amount of strain or fatigue involved and qualifications in terms of education, experience or training. The result of the analysis is a job profile, describing the scope of the job and the type of person required.

Once the job profile has been constructed it is possible to proceed to job evaluation which consists of ranking all the jobs within the organization in some particular order. The criteria on which this process is based will depend on the type of concern and the order will vary between firms, depending on which jobs are considered important.

Job evaluation and analysis set out the responsibilities involved in the performance of a particular job plus the information and resources required for its performance. Such information can serve as the basis of a system of job grading which can then be used as a foundation for a wage and salary structure.

8. Promotion

A feature of a company manpower policy must be planned promotion. The policy should be made clear to all employees and should specify the various promotional routes and the conditions attaching to each. While not every member of an organization may want promotion, it is essential for a company to foster the ambitions of those desire achievement and advancement and to give them all possible assistance in clarifying their own personal goals and matching these to company requirements.

The selection of those required to fill supervisory and higher posts is very important. In addition to technical competence, such posts require administrative ability and a knowledge and understanding of the organization as a whole. The holder of a supervisory post must possess qualities of leadership and the ability to command respect and co-operation.

Although a supervisor must possess a certain level of technical skill and knowledge of the processes or operations under his control, these qualities alone will not make an effective supervisor. It must be assumed that candidates for promotion are already in possession of the necessary technical competence.

There is a view that a person ceases to be promoted when it is shown he cannot adequately cope with his present job. If this is so, it obviously is conducive to inefficiency. 'In a hierarchy every employee tends to rise to his level of incompetence' (Laurence J. Peter 'The Peter Principle').

9. Transfers

It is not always possible to guarantee the complete suitability of an individual for a particular job. The personnel officer (who has, through the selection procedure, acquired a knowledge of the employee's capabilities) is best placed to recommend a transfer into a post where, for either personal or technical reasons, the employee may find more satisfactory work.

The employee represents an investment in both financial and organizational terms. Where the redeployment of labor becomes necessary, transfer is a better solution than outright dismissal. Again it is the personnel officer who can advise, interview, and persuade employees to accept a transfer.

10. Withdrawals

Retirements. The careful handling of those due to retire, so that they do not feel the undertaking is no longer interested in them, can do much to foster good relations with the remainder of the employees.

Termination. The personnel officer should see all employees who are to be dismissed. The reasons for dismissal should be put fairly and frankly to the employee so that he does not leave with a sense of injustice. Any discontent voiced by the employee may give the personnel officer a lead as to weaknesses in the organization or in the supervisors, thus permitting remedial action to be taken.

Redundancy. Trade Union agreements usually provide for the last employees to come to be the first to go. The lists of those to be dismissed are usually agreed with the men's representatives. The reasons for and the extent of the redundancy should be communicated to the representatives well in advance, so as to avoid the restlessness and the search for other jobs which rumors of redundancy, unless checked, can foster.

11. Labor Turnover

Some level of labor turnover may be considered natural wastage. This level should be kept low as employees cost money to recruit and train, and a high rate of turnover is a barrier to the development of the integrated working groups that are a precondition of efficient work. An increasing rate of labor turnover is usually indicative of some disturbance in the firm's labor relations and requires attention.

Human resources should continuously monitor labor turnover to guard against marked departures from the normal rate. To do this an index of labor turnover is required. This may be found by dividing the total number of leavers per unit time by the average number employed and expressing the resulting fraction as a percentage.

Care is needed in interpreting changes in the index. If for a monthly index a 5% turnover is regarded as normal then a series of successive monthly values like 5%, 6%, 5%, 4%, 7%, 5%, 3%, can be taken as being due to chance fluctuations and the deviations can be disregarded. However, values of 5%, 6%, 5%, 7%, 8%, 8%, showing a consistent upward trend, should not be ignored.

Reasons for an increasing or high rate of turn over may be either internal, e.g. bad working conditions, or external, e.g. strong local completion for labor.

12. Welfare

Most firms find that it is necessary to offer more than the minimum facilities required by law. With increasing social awareness of hygiene, health and general environmental factors, demands for suitable working conditions are growing. In addition, many studies have proved that a pleasant and human environment enhances efficiency and leads to greater attachment and loyalty to the work place. These factors have led employers to offer welfare measures on a competitive basis to present a better image of a particular firm and its employment circumstances.

However, the greatest scope for pursuing this policy of enlightened self-interest is in the field loosely described as welfare. Canteens (or their substitute, luncheon vouchers), social clubs, sport activities and organized holidays are in many cases financed by companies.

Employee counseling can have a beneficial effect on good human relations. If employees know that a welfare officer is available to whom they can talk confidentially about any personal problem and who is capable of giving advice and help, it tends to foster the conviction that management cares about the members of the organization.

13. Safety and Health

Management must provide and maintain safe working conditions within the undertaking, e.g. belts and pulleys must be securely fenced.

The duties of a works safety officer include:

a) Routine inspection of plant, buildings, gangways, etc.
b) Training employees and others in methods of safe working.
c) Ensuring that protective equipment and clothing are used where prescribed.
d) Advising on layout of plant, machinery, working conditions, etc., from the point of view of safety.
e) Creating an active interest in safety precautions and accident precaution by means of lectures, notices, etc.
f) Investigation of all accidents and making recommendation with a view to prevention of similar occurrences in the future.

14. Management by Objectives (MbO)

This is used in many companies in an attempt to substitute management by self control for management by domination. The personnel manager will frequently have the task of implementing and maintaining the system. MbO entails setting management, at various levels, individual targets to meet short and long term objectives. A manager agrees his proposed target with his superior and then performance is regularly assessed against the target when the opportunity is taken to amend the target if necessary. Not only should this motivate management to achieve set targets but it will also enable management to obtain a degree of job satisfaction. It will also indicate training needs and where delegation is necessary.

15. Staff reports

There must be a system of regular reports on each member of the staff. They should include not only details of the member's proficiency but also such personal attributes as have a relevance to his work. Such reports may be in essay form or may require the assessor to answer specific questions, often quantitatively. This is known as merit training. Amongst other objectives, the reports may indicate where further training is necessary, where promotion is justified, etc.

16. Staff records

These should include a sheet of card containing the basic information about the staff member and summary of his movements between the departments and between grades, with a record of his remuneration. Filed with it would be the original application form, staff reports and any relevant correspondence.

17. Wages and salaries Determination

The fixing of wages and salaries is the responsibility of top management. However, the human resource officer plays an important part in the bargaining process. Not only is he often management's chief negotiator, but he can also make an important contribution in formulating the company's wage and salary policy. Industry-wide bargaining is frequently replaced by productivity agreements, in which individual firms negotiate a compromise agreement where greater efficiency and productivity are assured through the modification of working practices by labor in return for substantial wage increases. Such agreements may involve planned redundancies amongst the labor force.

Ideally, staff payments should be based on a system of job grading. However, certain problems e.g. office overtime, often remain. Because of this, bonuses and increment payment are often paid, not on measured individual performance which is often very difficult to determine, but on total performance which is often very difficult to determine, but on total performance of a particular group or of the whole firm.

Attempts have been made in several instances to introduce profit-sharing or employee-share-holding systems, aiming at greater personal involvement with the company's fortunes and thus giving greater motivation to teamwork, but so far the benefits of such schemes have not proved to be of obvious advantage to either party.

18. Industrial Relations

This term refers to the more formal official relationships between groups or bodies with differing interests (i.e. employers' organizations, trade unions, the Government) and to relations between the management of a single firm and representatives of its work force.

Employers' organizations are usually formed on the basis of particular industries. Whilst they do have other functions e.g. making representations to government, co-operating in setting standards etc., their main task is the preparation and handling of nationwide or industry wide wage negotiations including fringe benefits, conditions of work, etc.

The trade unions have developed into integral social institutions, often with great influence on recruitment and training. Their primary function is the protection and advancement of their members' rights and interests. As a supplement to the unions, shop stewards, who are the direct first-line representatives of separate working groups, have gradually acquired great powers and responsibilities.

The groundwork for reasonable industrial relations lies in good two-way communication. While industrial conflict can and does arise from genuine differences of interests this is often overlaid by ignorance, insecurity, rumor and fear. By clarifying the issues honestly and maintaining a 'dialogue' between management and labor, personnel management can, if not avoid conflict, at least reduce it. This is often attempted by using a system of **Joint Consultation.** The term can refer to an arrangement within an industry by regularized meetings of trade union and employers' representatives or a committee within a firm.

PART THREE

THE PURCHASING AND MARKETING FUNCTIONS

THE PURCHASING FUNCTION

1. The Purchasing Department

THIS DEPARTMENT WILL be responsible for the buying of materials and components in the case of a manufacturing company and completed goods in the case of wholesaling and retailing organizations. The position of the Purchasing Officer will depend upon the type of business and the extent to which purchasing plays a part in the organization. In some businesses, such as those which provide only a service, purchasing would be a very minor function. In a manufacturing company the Purchasing Officer will have connections with the Production Department which will tell him the types and amounts of the purchases and the dates by which they must be available. In a selling organization he will be advised by the Sales Department of those goods which are expected to find a ready market. Thus, the first firm will buy according to known needs; the second firm will buy according to anticipated sales.

A large purchasing staff will usually be composed of specialists, each being knowledgeable in his particular field. Each officer would be aware of the various sources of supply, the superiority of one supplier over another as regards delivery times, and current and anticipated prices. Intimate contact with the supply market is therefore essential.

2. Purchasing Policy

This will take account of the following considerations:

a) To buy at the lowest price consistent with quality and delivery service.
b) To buy goods as required or to contract for purchases over a period. Contracting ensures a flow of supplies which can be geared to usage and gives an assurance of certainty. The effect of being tied to a price during the period of the contract will depend upon the trend of prices. To buy only when the goods are required may result in having to do so when prices are unfavorable and supply is uncertain. Such a method would be used if the goods were not in constant use, such as materials for 'one off' jobs.
c) In some businesses (relating to cocoa, copper etc.) buying is in 'futures'. That is, goods are bought at a price agreed today for delivery in the future. The possibility of an adverse movement in price must mean that such purchasing is speculative.
d) Buying may be centralized, whereby the purchasing for different factories, shops etc., is by the head office. This gives the advantage of being able to buy in larger amounts and so at lower unit costs. With a larger purchasing department there could be more specialization amongst the buyers; standardization of procedure and control could also be improved. Against this is that, in the case of purchases for sale, the branch would be more aware of local demand. Centralization can lead to delays in ordering and delivery—one of the disadvantages of a too rigid organization.

3. *Storage and stock Control*

This ensures that the items required for production or other use are available when required. Storage is necessary because there can be no absolute certainty of punctual deliveries of supplies but it must be recognized that storage is costly in terms of rent, depreciation, interest charges, labor etc. Stores management is therefore a compromise between cost reduction and the ensuring of uninterrupted production. Production wishes to have a wide margin of safety in terms of stock, whilst costing procedures attempt to reduce storage costs.

The following are essentials for efficient stock control:

a) The identification of stock by a system of coding, referenced to a manual of stock items.

b) Locating stock according to the frequency of use; the ease of handling; the demands of safety and security.
c) The establishment of safe limits of minimum and maximum amounts of stock in hand for each item. This will be decided by the rate of usage and the length of delivery times. (The period between placing an order and its delivery is known as lead time). This, if production uses 1,000 units per week and the lead time is four weeks, the absolute minimum of stock in hand before re-ordering will be 4,000 units.
d) A system of continuous inventory and the physical checking of stock with the records.
e) A method of recording goods ordered and goods received.
f) The issuing of stock on authorized requisitions.
g) Stock records and 'bin cards' to record stock held.

THE MARKETING FUNCTION

4. Introduction

'Marketing is the process of determining consumer demand for a product or service, motivating its sale and distributing it into ultimate consumption at a profit'. There must be a constant flow of information to the manufacturer about what the customer really wants. This is particularly important when production units are large and inflexible and a number of intermediaries stand between them and the ultimate consumer. Unless the right type of goods is made, they may prove unsaleable and the money sunk in their manufacture will be lost.

The size of an undertaking or an industry depends in the long run upon the quantity that can be sold. An important duty of management is therefore to forecast sales for a reasonable period ahead because upon this depends (a) the amount of finance necessary, and (b) the size of the investment in productive facilities and raw materials. It is therefore necessary for the management to consider the resultant of the three factors, sales, production and finance, for each depends on and affects the others. It is, for example, dangerous to endeavor to pursue a sales policy which cannot be matched by the productive facilities, or which makes excessive demands upon finance; nor can efficient and profitable production be carried out in a factory the capacity of which is substantially in excess of the demand made upon it.

5. The 'Marketing Concept'

During the early part of the twentieth century, industrial management was mainly production-oriented. The chief concern of businessmen was the solution of problems posed by the technological aspects of production and their primary aim was to cut costs.

Gradually more money has become available for expenditure on 'luxury' commodities and services. Buyers are more knowledgeable and discerning about their purchases, and goods have become more diverse in scope and more sophisticated. Consequently, the efforts of the marketing department become increasingly important. Techniques have been developed for ascertaining consumers' needs and it has become essential that these needs are considered in deciding the right balance of goods to make and sell.

This has led to the development of the 'marketing concept'. Firms put considerable effort into finding out what the customer wants—or is likely to want—as a preliminary to marshaling resources into designing, manufacturing, packaging and selling. Goods must be available at the prices consumers are willing to pay at the places they are wanted. Consumers must be continuously informed about the availability and advantages of specific products. Marketing is not just an extension and refinement of selling, but is part of the driving force of the whole organization. Important business functions, such as research, design, production, etc. are now primarily customer oriented.

6. *Marketing Policies*

Management must formulate the appropriate marketing policy for the firm. Individual markets must be assessed and decisions taken on what constitutes the optimum deployment of the company's resources.

Marketing objectives (e.g. the most profitable volume to be produced, whether or not to introduce new products etc.) must be set and the manner in which these objectives are to be realized (e.g. whether to supply the top end of the market with high priced quality goods, as against trying to capture a mass market with high priced quality goods, as against trying to capture a mass market and which channel of distribution to use). An important repercussion of marketing policy is on the company image that is created and maintained in the eyes of buyers and distributors.

The particular marketing policy must be consistent with the firm's resources and opportunities. It should be stable in the medium term so as to offer an adequate guideline to implementation, while being flexible enough to allow for any modifications.

7. *Market Planning*

The marketing aspect involves making a set of decisions on product types, prices, promotion and distribution upon which further action can be based. This constitutes the 'marketing mix', which is an essential guide for subsequent marketing actions. The plan must consider not only internal factors but also external ones, such as the state of demand, technological innovation, Government action, etc. Plans should be continuously controlled to ensure that they are properly carried out and to enable them to be modified. The usual form of overall control is the marketing budge, which represents the qualifying of marketing decisions in money terms.

The practical result of market planning is a particular marketing strategy such as:

i. A penetration strategy, aiming at a high volume of sales with a low level of profit per unit sold. This is suitable where a manufacturer has decided to sell in a mass consumption market. It involves building up and controlling a large sales force; inducing large numbers of distributors to keep the particular goods in stock; creating suitable packaging and spending large sums on advertising. This particular approach is invariably preceded by a lengthy period of product development, market testing and detailed market research.

ii. A segmentation strategy is often appropriate for those products whose market is not homogeneous. The manufacturer has the opportunity of offering the same product for sale with the opportunity of offering the same product for sale with certain minor modifications to suit the tastes of each particular group of consumers, e.g. the sale of the same model of car in various colors or with different optional extras.

Particular plans and strategies are dependent on availability of information on current market conditions. The risks involved are generally too great to launch a new product or to try to open up a new market without first assessing the potential as fully as possible by market research methods.

8. *Market Research*

Information must be collected and analyzed about the market and the customers. Manufactured articles must have intrinsic merit at an attractive price and must fit a particular market so as to prove acceptable to a sufficiently wide public and thus justify a steady flow of production. The Sales Management must find that market in the most direct and economical way, and must ensure that the goods are of the design, quality and price which will meet with wide acceptance.

Market Research is the collection and analysis of relevant data concerning specific products and their markets. The first stage is **Desk Research.** This is the evaluation of information already available and includes official reports, handbooks, Government and international publications, agency surveys etc.

The next stage is **Field Research.** This involves gathering information from actual or potential users and distributors of the proposed product.

It is essential to distinguish exactly which type of market is being analysed and to adapt the techniques used accordingly. The primary distinction is between industrial and consumer markets.

Industrial Markets. Here potential customers are fewer, buying decisions are governed by rational calculation and changes in taste are often slower than in consumer markets. The links between producer and user are usually close and more direct in industrial markets.

Surveys are fairly easy to conduct and the results usually reliable as a fair degree of co-operation can be expected, e.g. questionnaires sent through the post usually produce a good response. Reliable data can also be gained by personal interviews and demonstrations or 'user tests' where equipment is loaned to a prospective user for testing and comment.

Consumer Markets. Consumer field research is more complex due to the unstable nature of consumer buying patterns and the large numbers of individual customers involved. Purchasing decisions are governed by such non-rational factors as convenience, class, status, etc. Therefore, **quantitative research,** which provides data on what is happening, is by itself insufficient and must be supplemented by **motivation research**, i.e. to analyze why particular things are happening.

The basic needs of mankind being broadly tastes, habits and preferences tend to be governed by the overall social ethos and the norms of particular social groups. It becomes possible to classify consumers into groups usually according to criteria based on their income and other social factors.

Some widely used consumer research techniques are:

i) **Quantitative Surveys.** These are assembled on a continuous basis by large agencies for fast-moving mass-consumption goods—tobacco, food clothing, etc.—and showing volume trends and differential movements in various parts of a large market.
ii) **Attitude Surveys.** These incorporate an attempt to discern the motivation surrounding the purchase of certain emotionally 'loaded products, like baby foods, cosmetics, etc.
iii) **Consumer Panel.** May be 'shopping basket' type, where selected consumers are asked to keep diaries of purchases over a specified time or 'discussion group' type, where a guided exchange of opinions takes place.
iv) **Consumer Survey.** These are based on carefully designed questionnaires and statistical sampling methods, and involve interviewing a random sample of potential users of a product.
v) **Test marketing.** This consists of the selection of a small area—county town, local television area, etc.—and the limited selling of the product through the normal distribution channels with an accompanying advertising effort.
vi) **Retail Audit** which analyzes the sales of competing brands at selected shops and thus assesses actual consumer demand.

Consumer research techniques are generally complex, expensive and not 100% reliable. However, with mass-consumption goods where large investments are at stake, their use is inescapable. Whatever the type, form or complexity of a particular marketing research assignment its purpose must be clearly established. Unless the type of information that is required and its use are both clearly defined, it is impossible to select the best method for the enquiry or to make a estimate of its probable cost. Also, while a single survey may establish the basic facts about a product and its potential market, the full value of Market research can only be realized by regarding it as a continuous process. By monitoring the progress of a product throughout its life any changes that become necessary in design, manufacture or distribution can be carried out with the minimum of disruption.

Although some of the largest companies maintain their own market research departments, this is not the general practice, as investigations are usually only carried out at intervals. There are a number of well-equipped expert organizations who specialize in this work.

9. Promotion

This relates to all the efforts made to increase sales. It may include advertising and, in an indirect way, public relations.

In the **domestic** market it can rely more on an 'impulse-buying' effect and often combines advertising with price cuts, trading stamps, competitions, etc. It is useful for maintaining turnover in an already well-established product or for trying to break into the market with a new product.

Manufacturers of **industrial** products generally rely less on advertising and more on personal selling than manufacturers of consumer goods. Where advertising **is** used, however, the media most frequently employed are sales literature, direct mail, the technical press, and exhibitions. Consumer goods tend to use these media much less, their main promotional outlets being the daily and weekly press, television, and, when merchandising techniques are used, the shops and stores themselves. Because of the highly complex nature of advertising most companies develop their advertising strategies with the help of specialized agencies.

10. Advertizing

This is the process of inducing and stimulating sales. Its scope ranges from merely giving information of what is available, e.g. a railway time-table, to the hard selling approach, e.g. television advertisements.

Much has been written about the social purpose and value of advertising. It is claimed that an effective campaign reduces the cost of an article, hence leading to a reduction in price, because the cost of a campaign is more than offset by the benefits of large-scale production made possible by an expanded market.

The actual cost of an advertisement must be considered in relationship both to (i) the number of persons who are likely to see it and (ii) the number of those persons to whom the wares advertised make a particular appeal. Certain papers and periodicals are claimed to have a high proportion of readers in the middle and upper income groups, hence advertising space in these tends to be more expensive than in those periodicals which, although of comparable numerical circulation, appeal to the less wealthy classes. Many products are of little or no interest to the vast bulk of the population, appealing only to the special category of enthusiasts for a particular activity or hobby or to those in a particular part of the country. It is clearly wasteful to advertise such products in a journal of general appeal, as more potential buyers will be reached at less cost if advertising is concentrated in a journal catering for those special interests.

11. *The Advertising Budget*

The manufacturer must decide upon the size of his advertising budget and its division between the various media.

The factors which affect the size of the appropriation include the following:

a) Whether the product (or service) is now, well-established or declining.
b) The type of article.
c) The actions of competitors.
d) The availability, actual or potential, of the product.

The total amount to be spent on advertising is usually decided annually by the Board. Factors taken into account may be the amount sales, an assessment of the result of last year's advertising campaign, the advertising policy of competitors and the need to obtain increased sales in cases where a plant or department is not producing to capacity. The appropriation expressed as a percentage of sales varies widely in different industries.

The distribution of the total amount allocated for advertising is usually the responsibility of the Sales Manager or, in larger companies, the Advertising Manager, who should have regard to the following considerations:

i) Frequent changes of style or medium are unsatisfactory.
ii) Effort must not be scattered but must be concentrated upon that section of the public selected.
iii) The most appropriate media (e.g. Television, Press, Poster, Circulars) must be selected.
iv) Articles of narrow appeal should not be advertised in newspapers of wide circulation.
v) It is usually wiser, if funds are limited, to concentrate the campaign geographically, rather than to carry out a less intensive campaign over a wider area.
vi) The size of the advertisement should be adequate for the message to be conveyed, even if this means a less frequent appearance of the advertisement.

12. Pricing and Costing

Budgeting needs a consistent costing structure and established pricing policies. The lowest theoretical level at which selling prices can be set is determined by the firm's unit costs.

A trend which has emerged is the relative divergence of production costs and marketing costs. With the development of better and more closely controlled production methods, the trend has been towards reduced or at least stable production costs. However, there has been a steady increase in all the various components of marketing costs: salesmen's costs, advertising expenditure, costs of distribution both in the physical sense (packaging and transport) and in the cost of servicing distribution channels, and after-sales servicing, etc.

A firm's pricing policy is increasingly being recognized as one of the most important independent elements in the marketing mix. Policies need to be clearly worked out and involve a consideration of the whole mix in relation to prices: price and image, price and product quality, price and packaging, price and service and so on. The starting point for this consideration is the market, the prices customers are prepared to pay for the whole mix with varying emphasis on its different elements. Pricing, however, must be controlled by proper costing if it is to show optimum profit contribution over the whole life cycle of the product. A new product, for which demand is high, can command a 'premium' price, but once the mature period of its life cycle has been reached the price will tend to stabilize at a somewhat lower level. The prices charged by competitors and their reactions to the firm's own pricing policies will also have a bearing on the prices that are set.

13. Public Relations

The actions of a large company can make a significant impact upon substantial sections of the public, e.g. its shareholders, employees and customers and indeed upon the general public, as many of its actions possess a considerable news value. Large companies frequently employ a Public Relations Officer (P.R.O.) both to advise them upon likely public reaction to proposed courses of action and to be the means whereby the action is communicated to the organs of public information and interpreted in the most favorable light. A P.R.O. is usually an experienced journalist, possessing contacts in the television and newspaper world and capable of passing on material concerning the company's activities in a 'news-worthy' form.

14. Distribution

Distribution is the process of getting goods from the point of production to the point of sale. Involved are packaging, warehousing, transportation, handling and insurance. New technical developments—mechanical handling equipment, automated packing and the use of standardized containers for bulk carrying—offer alternatives to more traditional distribution methods. Costs can be cut and by allowing faster turnarounds with a greater safety, investment in packaging and insurance is reduced and a better utilization of capital promoted.

> i) **Industrial Markets.** Here the situation is relatively simple; about 50% of industrial products are sold directly by maker to user. However, with increasing standardization in this field, stock-holders or dealers are becoming more common. In the distribution of materials and supplies, raw and semi-finished materials, components, etc., distributors play a greater part as sources are often interchangeable and the quantities required may not warrant direct sales. This type of selling embraces the following:

a) Raw Materials. Where the materials are standardized, e.g. grain and metals, distribution will usually be effected through brokers or the appropriate Produce Exchange.
b) Components. Many manufacturers purchase some or most of the components in their products from specialized manufacturers, e.g. tires in the motor industry, bottles and containers in the cosmetic industry. The manufacturer must provide competent design and research facilities.
c) Services, e.g. Insurance, Advertising, Industrial Designers. The representative must understand the needs of his client and of the market in which he operates.
d) Equipment, machinery and transport. Besides supplying first-rate technical advice, the manufacturer must be able to provide prompt and reliable service in the event of breakdown or failure.
e) Sundries. Most household needs, e.g. paint, soaps and brooms, have their counterpart in the factory. It is usual to develop a special range of goods for industrial use, probably of a more robust nature and in large packs.

ii) **Consumer Markets.** Consumer distribution is more complex, with its variety of outlets, each of widely differing characteristics and effectiveness. This variety enables the manufacturer to choose the most appropriate distribution channel for his products.
The distributor has to make decisions on the range of different articles he is going to stock and display. Distributors may be:

a) general: carrying a wide assortment of lines with little variety within each line.
b) single-line: carrying a wide assortment of lines with greater variety within them.
c) specialized: carrying a clearly defined assortment with wide variety.

iii) **Wholesalers.** The rise of industrial giants, powerful retain groups, and the growing need for better and more direct communications between maker and user, has gradually restricted the wholesaler's role almost exclusively to commodity-type goods, e.g. food, simple clothing etc. This has meant that either the manufacturer

or the retailer has taken over the wholesaling function, thus giving both of them greater control over their marketing and production strategies.
iv) **Retailers** directly serve the individual buyer. Their variety is great and the range of efficiency differs widely. The main types are:

    a) **Independents:** single shops, or groups with not more than three outlets, have a comparatively low volume of sales and are associated with high profit margins and low efficiency. Although their numbers are decreasing their survival lies either in specialty fields or where highly personal service is important.

    b) **Department Stores:** By concentrating purchases under one roof, offering a wide assortment with a large variety and giving subsidiary services, they inaugurated shopping as a social activity and captured the custom of the rising middle classes. Their market share is, however, declining because they tend to have difficulties in the integration of departmental policies, with a consequent lack of flexibility.

    c) **Multiple or Chain Stores.** These concentrate on a narrow range of standardized, branded mass-consumption products. The principle of 'high turnover / low profit', centralized purchasing, better store location and layout policies led to their spearheading the 'consumer convenience' principle.

    d) **Co-operatives.** A poor image, unimaginative trading and inferior management led to their market share shrinking. Currently they are in the throes of large scale transformation through mergers and streamlining, as well as by improvements to their range of merchandise and selling techniques.

    e) **Mail Order Houses** have shown a fast growth rate. Mail order trading requires precise planning and efficient stock control, handling and sales administration techniques. As their range of products is limited, selection and pricing must be decided well in advance, while the cost of distribution, catalogue printing, mailing and postage can be very high.

    f) **Discount Houses.** These concerns are based on 'stripped price' selling, i.e. offering branded goods at reduced prices, 'stripped' of all customer service. There is usually no credit or delivery, the environment is bare, lines carried may vary and no after-sales service is offered.

v) **Voluntary chains.** The combination of one wholesaler and a large number of retailers in various trades has been quite successful. The wholesaler has a guaranteed turnover from the members who undertake to buy from him. In turn, the independent retailers enjoy some of the advantages of bulk buying, better store management, unified layout and a jointly established image. Buying Groups are similar groupings consisting of retailers only, who thus may use their joint buying power for better bargaining with suppliers.

vi) **Further developments.** Other wholesalers have set up Cash and Carry warehouses where retailers can collect supplies at competitive prices. The saving of transport, credit and sales costs allows keen pricing and gives small retailers the opportunity to reduce their own inventories. The system is suitable for fast-moving goods which are carried in limited varieties such as hardware, electrical goods, and packaged foods.

Large retailers use the strategy of own branding ('private label') where, owing to the superior buying power, manufacturers are induced to make goods under the store's name. The store, not having to carry the heavy promotional costs associated with branded goods, can therefore offer their own brands at lower prices than usual, relying on the shops' image to sell them.

15. Sales Management

This is a specialized application of the process of management as a whole. It calls for skill and resource in adapting a sales team to ever-changing circumstances and in constantly probing for new and more effective ways of finding and supplying the market. The duties of a Sales Manager are as follows:

i) Acting as a member of the Management Team in conjunction with the executives responsible for production and finance in deciding, or making recommendations, upon the sales policy of the business.

ii) The compilation of the sales and sales expenses budgets in collaboration with subordinate sales managers in charge of areas or products
iii) Leading and supervising the efforts of subordinate area and product sales managers in their task of achieving the sales budget.
iv) Keeping in touch with developments in public taste and changing market conditions and searching for and investigating new outlets for the company's products.
v) Except in larger businesses where there is probably an advertising manager, dealing with all matters relating to advertising, packing and display.
vi) Liaison with consultant firms specializing in market research and similar matters.
vii) Selection, training and control of the sales department.

16. The Sales Force

Buying a commodity is a personal decision; therefore, there is a need for personal salesmanship. The relative ignorance of customers in face of the increasing complexity of available goods and the growing demand for quality products means that advice on the detailed specifications of particular goods is frequently required.

The tasks of sales management begin with selection of salesmen. They must be people with sufficient self-discipline to work in isolation and must therefore have a high level of confidence both in their goods and in themselves. Their training must involve a thorough grounding in the working of the company, the products, the market and their competitors, as well as in the general techniques of handling customers.

Sales managers must assess and arrange potential customers according to their relative importance to the firm. A 'call-rate' is then calculated for the sales force—the number and frequency of visits to each customer—and the 'call costs'—which relate expenditure on the sales force to the realized sales volume. This will show which customers are large enough to warrant frequent visits and which it will be more economical to leave to wholesalers or other channels of distribution.

A sales force can be controlled by setting quotas or targets for individual salesmen. This procedure allows sales managers to implement management by exception, stepping in only where returns vary appreciably from set target figures. Where the territory covered is exceptionally large, the number of salesmen high, or technical content of the product demanding, the sales organization may be extended through appointing 'area managers' with delegated authority over part of the market.

17. Sales Forecasting

A specialized task of sales management is Sales Forecasting, the assessment of likely future trends i the movement of sales volumes. These assessments are based on analysis of past and present market information. Where markets are fairly stable with large-scale fluctuations unlikely to occur, smaller variations in demand may be reliably predicted using various statistical techniques. Where demand is unstable the subjective opinions of the sales force executives are needed to supplement objective calculations.

18. Delivery

The delivery department must ensure that the goods are delivered in good condition at the right time and to the right place. For some products, speed of service, including delivery, is essential; in others the selection of the cheapest form irrespective of speed may be necessary. Rail transport, though lacking the flexibility of road vehicles, may become increasingly competitive, especially where, by co-operation between seller and customer, a regular pattern of deliveries can be arranged. Road transport, provided that full loads can be made up and light running minimized, is economical, possesses great flexibility and provides a means of contact between supplier and customer.

19. After Sales Service

In some cases this will be performed by the retailer under agreement with the manufacturer, in other cases it will be carried out by the manufacturer. The requirements are:

i) adequate stocks of spare parts, for both current and discontinued lines
ii) qualified staff to perform the repairs and service work, and,
iii. a speeding and efficient service

The service department should keep records of work performed as:

i) they may be a guide to the design department;
ii) modifications may be introduced to reduce service work, and,
iii) they will be a guide for stock levels of spare parts.

20. Export Marketing

This follows similar rules to marketing at home, but with the qualification that trading is taking place across frontiers and over longer distances and that usually increased risks are involved.

Market Research overseas is often costlier and more difficult, owing to the greater problem experienced in obtaining data. However, desk research can establish whether or not there is a market in an overseas country. In field research, many of the facilities for data collection may be required, especially in assessing qualitative data on cultural and social factors which can have a profound influence on a firm's marketing prospects. This means that personal visits to the selected markets are normally essential to identify such intangibles as the prevailing business climate.

Product policies often need modification because of the varying requirements of foreign markets, the most typical being the language difference and the need for appropriate technical specifications. Distribution is more complicated when exporting owing to the larger time intervals and greater distances involved. Agency support is important in overseas promotion in order to assess, select and successfully use media, exploit opportunities at the point of sale, adopt the best style of packaging, etc.

The tendency is to charge different prices in each market depending on the relative rate of demand, the place of the product in the customer's priorities, the need for technical support, and the use of credit as a marketing tool. Additional cost factors such as transport, insurance and tariffs will influence the competitive situation.

Export policies require that a separate approach is made to each overseas market so as to assess the best balance of the marketing mix, to survey trading policies of overseas Government, habits of purchasers, customs of distributors, etc.

Many firms find it advantageous to export capital and knowhow rather than goods. This is usually done by setting up overseas subsidiaries and thus becoming part of the social and economic fabric of that country.

The main functions of an export department are:

a) A shipping department to deal with the frequently complicated problems of shipping documents, insurance, currency and import restrictions, quotas, etc.
b) A packing department to see to the appropriate packing of the goods and the marking of cases, bales, etc.
c) An export sales department to deal with the many varieties of foreign habits, fashions, sizes, etc., which must be taken into account in manufacture.

21. Product Development

Rapid technological change, increasing sophistication of consumers and growth of competition between firms, all make it necessary for successful concerns to work on the development of new products. While existing products can be used as a basis, there are often limits to the amount of adapting, modernizing or repackaging that can be done. New products are developed as a result of (i) inventions or discoveries within the firm's research department, (ii) the purchase of patents representing new inventions, (iii) the taking over of smaller innovating firms.

Successful product development demands proper co-ordination of the company's resources. The organizational shape of this combined effort is usually a 'Product Development Committee' consisting of members from each of the functional departments.

An important factor when deciding whether or not to launch a new product is the concept of a product life cycle, i.e. the movement of expected sales over time, related to both production costs and profits over the same period. After the initial appearance of the product the growth of sales may be expected to be only gradual. Then, as its attractions become more widely known, the sales curve starts to rise sharply. At this stage competition becomes an important factor as direct imitations or slightly different goods aimed at the same section of the market are introduced. At this period of 'maturity', with the product being widely accepted, the firm's aim is to stabilize the situation with settled market shares for itself and its competitors and a predictable volume of sales.

Gradually, as the product loses its novelty, value devices such as branding are needed to ensure that it still remains in the public's consciousness. The final stage is when the product has lost favor sufficiently to be replaced.

The aim of the firm's marketing strategy must be to ensure that in the initial period of the 'life-cycle' the product quickly establishes a strong position to withstand competition. In this strategic process the whole marketing mix is involved. Thus the initial price is probably set fairly high and may have to be altered while changes are rung on advertising and sales promotion. Predicting the life-cycle—especially for new untried products—can be difficult, requiring careful market investigation and complex techniques for data analysis.

PART FOUR

THE PRODUCTION FUNCTION

1. Introduction

PRODUCTION IS THE essential function of making things. It is the process whereby materials are transformed for human use. For analytical purposes, the different types of production are conventionally classified into Agriculture, Fisheries, Mining, Industrial, and Services. It is, however, difficult to draw rigid distinctions between each of these categories. In the main, the basic technology of the first three has changed relatively less quickly than that of Industrial production, whilst it is only comparatively recently that the service industries have achieved their present importance.

A spur to technological advance in industrial production has been the complexity of the problems involved and the correspondingly large rewards obtainable by solving them. Research, production policy, purchasing and stock control etc. all involve separate techniques, and all must be welded together by management for the common purpose of producing goods and services for the market.

2. Production Policy

a) **General.** Production policies aim at providing answers to the problems of what commodities are to be produced, the manner of their production, volume and timing. The answers to these questions will depend both on the manufacturing **objectives** of the company, i.e. what should be achieved in its given market over a fixed time period at what cost and profit, and on its **resources**—machinery and buildings, manpower, market standing etc.

Each company must decide on a limited range of products or services, which it is able to produce at a competitive price, which provides an acceptable level of profit and which suits the range of skills and facilities available to the firm. Once these broad guidelines have been established, production policy has to provide the basis for a vast number of detailed decisions, e.g. the 'mix' of individual items, the materials and components required, whether to buy these or make them, what manufacturing processes to use etc.

On the basis of these factors, detailed planning must take place and standard control procedures set up, to enable actual performance to be checked against these plans.

b) **Production Engineering.** This is defined as the attempt to secure desired quality in optimum quantity at permitted cost. It is concerned with the total production process: the nature and use of the product, location, design and layout of productive facilities, handling methods, levels of mechanization and automation, organization of manpower, supervision and inspection etc. Thus production engineering embraces the whole period of time during which decisions taken currently will be effective. The importance of this stems from the increasing time horizon needed for planning decisions under conditions of growing investment requirements. In many industries planning must look 5-10, or more, years ahead. Production Engineering has the task of supplying the data and its analysis in technical terms for long-range planning.

c) **The 3 'S's.** Some of the principles applied by Production Engineering are:

   i) **Simplification** is the reduction of unnecessary variety. The ideal situation is where large quantities of a product can be made by means of an unchanging process, thus leading to 'economies of scale'.

   ii) **Standardization** is the control of necessary variety. A standard is set of acceptable rules according to which articles, processes or procedures should be made or regulated. Standards may apply to quality, strength, size, composition, or any feature of importance. Most standards also incorporate permissible variances as absolute perfection is unattainable.

iii) **Specialization** is the concentration of effort on what one knows best. It is logical for the manufacturer to apply most of his resources to a comparatively narrow range of products where the special skills, machinery, proven materials etc. already exist. It puts an increasing strain on the coordinative efforts of management, who have to bring a very wide range of specialist activities together for a common purpose.

d) **Diversification.** Market changes, technological obsolescence and similar developments may place firms in the position of having spare productive capacity. These resources frequently have potential for development away from the existing range of activities. This plus the existence of new, competitive processes which may otherwise be thought of as endangering the standing and prospects of the company, may force the firm to try to turn its assets to other than traditional uses.

Diversification may originate in the production process itself as an alternative use of existing resources or as a result of market pressures requiring products which may not be a part of the original specialization of the firm.

As this is likely to involve either venturing into markets which are new to the company or adopting processes in which expertise is lacking, diversification is likely to be associated, at least initially, with problems of investment, skilled manpower, re-organization and research.

3. *Types of Production*

The organization of product systems depends on:

i) the process by which individual products are made;
ii) demand, which indicates product types and quantities;
iii) the firm's resources, which define the production alternatives.

According to these factors, production processes can be classified into three broad categories:

i) **Job** product is the making of the product either singly or in very small quantities, usually according to the buyer's specifications. Thus each individual product is a 'one-off' job.
In large-scale jobbing industries—civil engineering, building, shipbuilding, etc.—the sales process is often tied to a system of tendering. This is especially true of complicated public projects (roads, airports, complete factories, etc.), whereby the prospective purchaser issues a set of specifications for which he invites competitive price and delivery schedules. These often involve complex credit and financing arrangements and highlight the crucial importance of cost control in jobbing production.

ii) **Batch** production is where goods are produced in largely identical form in quantities known in advance. Here production is repetitive but limited. It is used where demand is intermittent or seasonal. The organization of batch production needs a considerable amount of pre-planning, standardization and manufacturing for stock in expectation of sales.
Batch production benefits from the interchangeability of components over a range of difficult products.

iii) **Flow or Line Production.** Each unit travels along a line from machine to machine. At each stage only a single operation is performed, until it appears at the end of the line as the fully finished product. In flow production, there will be the same number of machines as operations, and thus these machines will be single-purpose, performing the same task all the time in a constant manner. This has the advantage that the labor used can often be unskilled or trained to perform one particular action only. The system has a built-in self-control in that each operation depends on the previous one. Flow-production lines frequently use the moving conveyor-belt system, where the work-unit travels along an assembly-line whilst the various components are added and the necessary operations performed on it. Flow production depends on the existence of a stable demand with relatively little seasonal fluctuation.

(**Mass production** merely means any large-scale production).

4. Factory Location

Factors which may determine the site include the following:

a) Availability and suitability of the land and its access to transport facilities. Cost may be influenced by the level of local rates and the existence of any Government aid.
b) Availability of labor of the type required—e.g. skilled workers; part-time women worker's etc. The competition of other local employers must be considered.
c) Local regulations about planning permission, pollution, etc.

5. Factory Layout

The two main methods are:

i) Process layout. The plant is laid out so that a product will pass easily through its various stages, keeping to its own production line.
ii) Process layout. Plan is grouped according to its function and different products can be processed on the same machines in some instances.

The following additional points need consideration:

i) Machine space must allow for moving machine part
ii) adequate gangways for transporting materials, for human traffic;
iii) strong floors, for heavy machinery;
iv) accessibility to machines for servicing and safety devices.

6. Estimating

It is frequently necessary to arrive at a price for quoting purposes, especially in those undertakings which manufacture to customers' requirements. Such an estimate must be as accurate as possible for the following reasons:

i) Under-estimating leads to losses.

ii) Over-estimating leads to loss of business, with consequent shrinkage in turnover and profits.

The following steps are usually necessary:

a) The exact ascertainment of what the customer needs, bearing in mind that this may be different from what the customer has asked for.
b) The assembly of the essential technical data, e.g. dimensions, clearances, sizes, electrical supply voltage.
c) The costs of the necessary raw materials, parts, tools, labour and processes must be ascertained.
d) The physical limits of the factory and its plant, e.g. maximum lifting capacity of cranes, the swing of lathes, must be considered.
e) Co-operation with other departments, e.g. Methods Engineers, or Sales Department.
f) The ascertainment of the earliest delivery data, taking into account other contracts passing through the factory and the availability of raw material and labor.
g) The loading to be added to the factory cost to cover:

   i) Works overheads.
   ii) Administrative overheads.
   iii) Selling overheads
   iv) Profit

7. *Preliminary Planning*

As soon as an order is received or a decision has been taken to commence production of standard articles, production must be planned.

Note the following points:

i) Customers' orders. A careful record must be kept of the customers' needs so that if a repeat order is received, time is not lost in turning up notes and specifications.
ii) Stocks of Material and Parts. Stocks must be so large that they make excessive demands on storage space and finance nor so small

that the production is interfered with should delivery take longer than expected.

iii) Capacities and operation times. It is essential to have readily available the plan required and production times for all products, parts and assemblies, so that delivery dates can be computed and any bottlenecks exposed. In order to be able to calculate how long a certain order will take to pass through the factory a record of the plant and machinery and its capabilities must be maintained, so that an undue load is not placed upon a particular machine. Due allowance must be made for breakdowns, maintenance and setting-up times when computing the capacity.

iv) Orders on hand. If manufacture is for stock, records of finished products will be kept by the Sales Department who will requisition on the Production Department when stocks approach the minimum levels. In other cases, the Production Planning Department must be advised of orders on hand and of the delivery dates promised. These dates should not have been fixed without reference to the Production Planning Department. Completed orders should be marked off so that the balance of outstanding orders on the factory can be readily determined.

8. *Production Planning and Control*

This is defined as the maximum utilization of resources by determining the nature and place of work, and the time and method for doing it. Design specifications and sales forecasts furnish the framework for short—and medium-term plans.

Production Planning and Control (P.P.C.) may often exist in an advisory or 'staff' relationship with factory management. In co-operation with the latter, it prepares the plans and monitors production but has no direct control over personnel and their day-to-day activities.

First, the most suitable process is decided upon. Then schedules are constructed, establishing the logical sequence of operations from raw materials and components to the finished product stage. Next, time schedules will be set up according to the length of time required for each operation. This will be followed by loading—the precise and detailed allocation of particular tasks to each machine and working group.

Performance must be continuously checked and monitored. This process is called progress control and is operated by progress chasers who feed back information about deviations, materials shortages and bottlenecks.

There are a number of standard documents which are used as planning and control tools:

    i) Flow-charts, indicating the physical sequence of operations;
    ii) Materials Lists, which specify quantities of materials and components for each product;
    iii) Machine Loading Charts, giving the sequence of different work one by the same machine;
    iv) Inspection Schedules, setting out the places, times and criteria to be applied.

P.P.C. will be applied differently according to the nature of the work and the type of production involved. In jobbing production, pre-planning is difficult as detailed planning can only begin once orders are received. It is perhaps most complicated in batch production due to the many variables affecting each product and production centre. In flow production, planning must begin, ideally, before the factory is built as this must be completely suited to the process. Once the details have been decided upon, any further change will be difficult because of the cost and the lost time involved.

Just as no sharp dividing lines exist between the various types of production so it is not possible to associate the different types exclusively with different volumes of output. Jobbing production often includes items which are made on a batch basis, while batch-production frequently contains 'one-off' jobs. This is also possible for flow production, e.g. in development work. Similarly, jobbing production can range from the largest scale—tower blocks, bridges, etc.—to the design and manufacture of tiny single units. A batch can be anything from a few hundred units to a million, while flow production can operate on one machine along, producing small quantities only. In fact, the three types—job, batch and flow—can be viewed as a historical progression. Ideally, every manufacturer will try to upgrade his production system by converting individual jobs into batches and batches into continuous production.

It is essential that production planning and control be kept flexible so as to be able to utilize the most economical production form, depending on the prevailing circumstances, market forces and the firm's resources.

9. Inspection

It is inevitable that a certain percentage of products made will be faulty, i.e. not stricly conforming to the standards set. Inspection attempts to maintain prescribed standards, within the permissible limits of variation allowed, by eliminating the substandard items. Inspection should ensure the success of marketing, as the customer expects a certain quality (often associated with a brand name) and inspection can make reasonably certain that he will be satisfied.

The process of inspection involves setting the limits of permissible variation in the product. In engineering terms such are called **tolerances,** and are laid down in the design. The size of the permissible variation will vary according to the type of product ant the use to which it is put. This also applies to the methods used for inspection.

Inspection falls under the following heads:

a) **Inspection of Raw Material** by the appropriate tests to ensure that each purchase possess the attributes stipulated.
b) **Inspection of Work in Progress,** to see that it confirms to specification of quality. The earlier in the process of manufacture the faults are discovered the easier it may be to rectify them, and further expense in processing an already faulty article may be avoided.
c) **Process Control.** This is necessary in many industries to ensure that the predetermined conditions of manufacture are adhered to.
d) **Running Tests,** ensure that the product will perform satisfactorily under conditions in which it will be expected (i.e. by the purchaser) to operate.
e) **Statistical Quality Control.** It is usually impossible for the inspection staff to examine every process every day or every article produced. Accordingly, samples of material from each batch or each production run are drawn for inspection, either at random or at agreed intervals (e.g. every hundredth article produced). In

a similar manner certain processes will be examined each day or week, so that each is covered within an agreed period of time.

10. *Materials Handling*

Raw materials, components, semi-finished parts and completed goods all have to be moved, either from storage to the production line or between different parts of the factory. Whilst this is inevitable, it is also costly, both in time and in energy. Therefore, it is important to simplify and standardize such movements as far as possible.

Good handling facilities depend on the **layout** of the factory and the stores. Ideally, these should be designed to facilitate handling by avoiding undue distance between any two centers. In practice, the actual layout will be governed by the nature of product and the process.

Wherever possible, handling processes should be incorporated into the production line itself. This can sometimes be done by using overhead conveyors, moving assembly belts etc. Where this is impossible, handling should be considered organizationally as a specialist activity, and direct production workers should not be involved in it.

Automation can also contribute greatly to the solution of handling problems in specific circumstances, e.g. directing and controlling the flow of liquids in an oil refinery.

A general classification of handling equipment is:

a) for moving between two fixed points—conveyor belts, overhead trolleys, cranes etc.
b) for vertical movement between floors—gravity chutes, magnetic hoists etc.
c) for moving between non-fixed points—forklift trucks etc.

11. *Maintenance*

The purpose of maintenance is to ensure the correct functioning of all machinery and equipment. The governing principle should be prevention rather than first-aid, in order to avoid breakdowns and holdups as far as possible. This involves **planned maintenance,** where every machine or piece of equipment is regularly checked. A **maintenance schedule** should state how frequently each machine should be checked, corrected or conditioned and by this means **routine** maintenance can be established which will interfere as little as possible with production work. This scheduling will require careful planning and strict control, with the responsibility for each maintenance task clearly assigned.

By observing the trends of maintenance costs a scrapping schedule can be prepared, showing when given items of equipment will need to be replaced as their maintenance costs increase beyond acceptable limits.

Good maintenance requires attention at the design stage of the factory layout so that machines are easily accessible. Dismantling facilities must be planned and the necessary tools and materials properly stocked.

12. Maintenance Control Department

The responsibility of this department is to ensure that a supply of the right materials of the required quantity is available when needed.

Scheduling the supply is vital to ensure that not only are the materials to hand when required but also that they are not stored an undue time. Idle materials tie up capital and are costly in storage space. The scheduling is a complicated operation because account has to be taken of the rate of materials usage as determined by the anticipated production ratge and of the delivery periods of the suppliers.

The reduced cost of large scale purchasing must be set against the cost of storing materials not immediately usable.

13. Work Study

The term embraces two distinct yet interdependent groups of techniques, (i) Method Study and (ii) Work Measurement.

The former is carried out in order to improve method of production, whilst the latter assesses human effectiveness.

i) **Method Study.** In carrying out a method study the following steps are usually necessary:

   a) The existing conditions and methods must be recorded in detail, with the assistance of charts, graphs, photographs or films.
   b) The detailed record must be critically examined and the job analyzed in to its elementary movements.
   c) The person carrying out the study should ask himself at every stage of the operation:

      1) What is to be achieved and why is it necessary?
      2) Where is it done and why there?
      3) When is it done and why then?
      4) By whom is it done and why that person?
      5) How is it done and why in that way?

   d) Any operation which cannot be justified in the light of this examination is either eliminated altogether or superseded by one which can.
   e) The method should be reduced to a written standard practice and any variations for the method must be corrected or incorporated in the process layout.

ii) **Work Measurement.** The results of this evaluation are used in the following directions:

   a) Operation planning and control
   b) Manning of plant and equipment
   c) Installation and operation of incentive schemes
   d) Comparison between different methods of working.

In carrying out a study, an understanding of the human factors involved is essential as the techniques, particularly time study, frequently give rise to annoyances or resentment.

The results of time study can be expressed either in terms of time (e.g. 'Standard Minutes') or of 'Work factors:

a) Variations between operations
b) Increasing fatigue as the day or shift proceeds.
c) Unavoidable delays inherent in the task, special or adverse working conditions or material.

The **standard time** is therefore based on the normal time it is considered the task should take when the operator concerned maintains a particular standard of performance as an average over the whole day.

The techniques of work measurement are as follows:

a) **Direct Time Study,** by means of recording at different times and in respect of different operations, of the time taken to perform a particular element of a given task, usually of a repetitive nature.
b) **Synthesis,** or the obtaining of data of times for the repetitive sub-elements of a job which is itself not a repetitive nature.
c) **Analytical Estimating,** by a trained estimator, of the length of time the non-repetitive parts of a task should take so that a standard time can be evaluated for the complete task.
d) **Predetermined Motion Time System,** sets times for the duration of basic movements under varying conditions.
e) **Activity Sampling,** whereby a 'random observation study' is made to record what is taking place on a job at particular moments over a representative period of time.

14. *Value Analysis*

The practical application of this technique is known as value engineering.

The purpose is to identify in detail the function of each part of a manufacturing process. From this examination a study is made of the most economical way of performing that function by, for example, introducing substitutes, changing the process, buying a component instead of making it, etc. The study goes back to the design stage instead of commencing from that point.

The method differs from other cost-reducing techniques by first considering the function of each part and then considering the cost. By evaluating the individual importance of each element and applying fresh though to the possibility of alternatives, value analysis aids cost reduction and encourages management to concentrate on the ability to innovate. Where necessary, emphasis would be given to the more costly parts of a process.

15. Automation

This refers to a method of operating automatic machines by an external impulse other than a human one. Computers, for example, can be programmed to activate machines through a series of processes or a series of machines. Such a system would include automatic check and control so that deviations and malfunctions would be automatically corrected.

16. Ergonomics

Sometimes known as human engineering, this is the study of man in relations to his working environment. It can relate to the environment generally—the effect of temperature, noise, etc.—but it is more commonly related to physical posture. There has been built up a study leading to the better design of chairs and the improved positioning of foot and hand controls on machines with the object of reducing physical strain.

17. Research

In an industrial context, this usually means the advance of scientific knowledge aimed at developing new products or providing the means for improving old ones. This may be done by evolving better processes, new materials, or new sources of energy. More recently, however, research has become an important element in practically every field of management and in the form of Marketing Research, Behavioral Research etc. has made an enormous contribution to management's ability to run the modern business organization successfully.

Scientific research can be divided into:

   i) Fundamental (or Pure) Research, whose purpose is to extend the frontiers of knowledge, with no immediate practical application in view.

ii) Applied Research, which is aimed at a particular practical use.

Firms, especially larger ones, in the science-based industries—aircraft, drugs, electronics etc.—often engaged in fundamental research in the hope either of obtaining an important 'breakthrough' which can be turned to direct commercial advantage or of obtaining technological 'fail out', or results peripheral to the main line or research but which turn out to be of value (sometimes known as 'spin off'). However, such breakthroughs are relatively infrequent and unpredictable. Thus the majority of fundamental research consists of patient, gradual work, aimed at leading to better understanding of the physical world and is, therefore, of direct use only in the long term.

The long term horizon of most fundamental research together with the uncertainty of the eventual payoff means that the main field of research in industry is **applied research.** This is specifically directed towards the improvement, modification or refinement of existing knowledge, with a view to its commercial possibilities. It can take the form of improving methods or processes, reducing cost, discovering new materials and finding new uses for present products or by-products.

18. Development

The results of research are mainly theoretical, being based on laboratory or pilot tests. To ensure that what works on a test bench can also be manufactured by normal production efforts at acceptable cost, industry needs to establish a continuous program of testing, evaluation, modification and correction in close co-ordination with the research effort.

Development processes vary greatly according to the nature of the product and its market. Testing may be done in the laboratory, on test rigs or in special installations, by the use of marketing models or prototypes, or by 'user-testing' which consists of allowing potential users to give the product a trial and asking them to evaluate its performance.

Whatever method or methods are selected it is essential that sufficient detailed performance data is collected so as to provide information on probable manufacturing costs, on the feasibility of manufacturing the product with the firm's existing facilities, or alternatively, whether additional investment will be necessary. The fault-finding procedure will also throw up valuable information about the handling, care and maintenance of the product in its commercial life.

19. Design

The function of design is to create a detailed physical specification for a product. Its importance lies in the fact that the shape, size, wieght, appearance etc. of a product are all factors that will influence consumers' purchasing decisions. From the production point of view the aim of the designer is to reach an acceptable compromise between what is ideal and what is feasible. He must consider how the product can best be fitted to this firm's existing resources and how its distinctive features can properly be emphasised while still keeping its cost within reasonable limits.

i) **Formal, or aesthetic, design** applies solely to the appearance of the product, which with most consumer goods is of paramount importance. Prospective purchases are often judged by whether they are found to be pleasing to the eye. In fashion industries formal design is more important than any other single quality and may often decide the success or otherwise of the product.

From the point of view of the manufacturing organization, once a particular product design has been finalized it becomes 'frozen', i.e. the product has to be made in this and no other way. It thus becomes a standard from which no deviation is desirable in the short term. In the longer term, however, design must be sufficiently flexible to allow for modifications dictated by changes in the underlying factors of fashion and technological innovation. The importance of this aspect of design lies in the decisions about the structure of the production process that depend on it, the materials and processes that are to be used, the costs associated with them etc.

In certain industries, the customer may initiate a design by asking for a product to be made according to his own specifications. For simple products, design can be evolved by the production personnel. For more complex ones, a number of draughtsmen may work at fixing the specification for every part or component. Alternatively, an outside design consultancy or the services of a freelance creative designer may be employed.

As their activities are to a large extent interrelated, Research, Development and Design are often placed under the same overall direction. In addition, the function of Inspection is frequently subordinated to Design. This ensures the independence of inspectors from operating production.

PART FIVE

THE ADMINISTRATIVE FUNCTION

1. Introduction

'ADMINISTRATIVE MANAGEMENT IS that branch of management which is concerned with the services of obtaining, recording and analyzing information, of planning and communicating, by means of which the management of a business safeguards its assets, promotes its affairs and achieves its objectives'—The Institute of Administrative Management.

It is, therefore, a service in that it obtains, processes and provides information. As such it is concerned with:

a) **Organization.** The planning of work must aim to ensure speed and accuracy. This will entail the organization of personnel as well as the creation of systems.
b) **Cost effectiveness.** Of itself it must be economical and it must also aid in the reduction of costs **generally** by increasing efficiency.
c) **The human factor.** No matter how mechanized an office may be, management requires leadership, judgment and human understanding.

2. Office Organization

Most clerical operations are simple if viewed in isolation. Office work, however, is concerned with a complexity of interrelated clerical operations and involves the following:

a) **Planning.** The most elementary operation entails a degree of planning; at the other extreme it is of such a magnitude as to demand a scientific approach.
b) **Co-ordination.** In any office system, a piece of work will pass through more than one stage, requiring the construction of a procedure.
c) **Specialization.** As a consequence of the above, there will be specialization of work at the different stages.
d) **Control.** The efficiency of the system must be checked on and, as a business is constantly changing, revised as appropriate.

3. Servicing Departments

Apart from the specialist functions of any one office, there are services common to all of them. These may be summarized as follows:

a) **Communications**—correspondence (typing, mail etc.), telephones, telex, messengers, etc.
b) **Reprographic systems.**
c) **Filing.**

These are routine activities, continuously in being, which are essential adjuncts to the work of any office. On their efficiency depends the ability of the office to carry out its functions effectively.

Support services are made available to any department requiring specialist assistance whenever the need arises. These could include the Human Resources and Legal Departments, for example.

4. Centralization of general services

All services continuously employed by all are capable of centralization but whether it would be advantageous to do so would depend upon the particular circumstances. Centralization can have the following **advantages**:

a) Overall costs of personnel space and equipment would be reduced. Each factor would be more fully employed because of the increased flexibility.

b) Because less equipment would be duplicated, more sophisticated equipment could be afforded.
c) The accommodation could be designed to suit the specialized requirements of the centralized services.
d) Increased specialization by staff would improve efficiency

The **disadvantages** could be:

a) Loss of personal pride and interest.
b) Delays in not having the service immediately available.
c) Unsuitability for confidential and very specialized work.

5. Organization and Methods

The complexity of work-planning in an office, other than for the simplest of operations, is such as to warrant scientific study. Because of their inter-dependence, there must be co-ordination of office tasks. This network, in its turn is part of the organization structure of the business.

Organization and methods (sometimes known as **work simplification**) is a scientific study of the most effective way of carrying out a clerical procedure and as such it is the province of specialists. Accordingly, in a sizeable organization the Organization and Methods Department is a **servicing** department in that its expertise is available throughout the organization. Its range of activities would include not only the drafting of procedures but would also encompass machines, equipment, forms, etc., and the re-allocation of staff.

6. Organization and Methods (O&M) in Operation

An O & M assignment will, in most cases, entail the revision of an existing system—either to make it more efficient or to extend it to cope with new circumstances.

A summary of the stages of such an assignment is as follows:

a) **Determine the purpose.** This must be clearly established at the outset and should be expressed in the form of written instructions.

b) **Analyze the current procedure.** It must be determined **what** is to be done, **how** it is done, **where, why** and **by whom** it is done. This will require an overall examination of the procedure; a study of the work of each operative; the forms used. The result may be expressed in a series of notes and/or charts. From this could be observed any duplication of effort, unnecessary operations, bottle-necks, areas of potential error, unjustified cost etc. So far as possible the results should be **quantitative**—e.g. number of forms; processing time; staff employed and cost; frequency of error etc.

c) **Re-design.** The proposed new procedure is drawn up. This will indicate the new method of operation, the forms to be used, any re-arrangement of staff which may be necessary and quantitative estimates for comparison purposes.

d) **Submit.** The proposals are usually submitted to the departmental managers concerned before being sent to the management for approval.

7. *Charting*

These are graphic representations of various work processes, the major ones being as follows:

Work scheduling. This is a program of work to be done, either as a regular practice over a standard period (e.g. dispatch of monthly statements) or for an occasional job (e.g. stocktaking). It is a timetable to ensure (a) the completion of the operation within a set time; (b) the availability of staff and equipment at each part of the time scale.

Process chart. This presents all the operations within a procedure and their sequences. Symbols are used to indicate the type of each operation—e.g. hand operation, machine operation, storage, transport etc.

Procedure flow chart. This indicates the flow of paper from one work point to another. It is particularly useful when a number of copies of one form are routed to different times of the day or week.

Production or output control. This is the measurement of the output against standard of output; (b) indicate the fluctuations of work as between different times of the day or week.

8. Mechanization

Machines are used to:

a) **Save time.** Firstly, there is the obvious fact that a machine can calculate and/or produce records quicker than is possible by hand. Secondly, a machine can perform several operations simultaneously and produce different forms of data from the same basic information.

b) **Reduce labor costs.** A machine will do the work of several manual operators but the comparison must be of the **cost,** as a machine operator would probably command a comparatively high salary. On the other hand, much machine work is routine and this could result in a proportion of the staff being lower paid.

c) **Give greater accuracy.** The sophistication of machines is such that accuracy can be relied upon. This is subject to the qualification that the basic data and the instructions to be fed in first must be by human action.

d) **Provide uniformity and legibility.** The problems of varying and sometimes and handwriting are eliminated.

9. Limitations of mechanization

a) The expense of a machine is justified only if it is employed to an economic extent. Normally, using a machine for only part of the day would still justify its cost but below a certain level of usage it may be unduly expensive.

b) The introduction of a machine may necessitate considerable alterations to the existing office systems. It could be that the consequent disruption and expenses would make installation unjustified.

c) A machine should, where possible, be flexible in its application. At a later date it may be required for a machine to produce an increased amount of data or produce data in more forms. If it is unable to be adjusted it will become obsolete.

d) Skilled operators are not always readily available.
e) To the cost of the machine may have to be added the continuing expense of specialized stationery.
f) Machine breakdown or power failure can cause problems.

10. Electronic equipment

The distinguishing feature is that the motive power is electronic instead of mechanical. Apart from the increased speed of operation, this makes possible the use of 'programs' which dictate the sequence of operations desired. The program and the basic data to be fed in can be stored on punched cards or tapes or on magnetic records.

11. Computers

The functions of a computer may be summarized thus:

a) To be controlled by one or more programs, some of which can be planned to intervene at different stages.
b) To receive data from one or more input sources.
c) To store information until required to be brought into the processing or for later reference.
d) To perform arithmetically.
e) To employ checks on the input and output data.
f) To produce visual results as determined by the program.

'Hardware' refers to the equipment; 'software' refers to programs. 'Packaged programs' are standard programs which can be used for such operations as payrolls, stock control etc.

12. Methods of filing

The essentials of a filing system are (a) accessibility; (b) ease of location; and (c) security.

The main classification of methods are as follows:

a) **Pigeon holes.** These can be used for (i) pre-sorting into first-letter order for subsequent strict alphabetical filing; (ii) sorting mail; (iii) storing catalogues etc.
b) **Lever arch.** This provides for retention of papers in book form. Papers must be punched and are held by a lever. It is suitable for filing standard forms—if these are numbered they can be kept in numerical order by inserting into the correct positions.
c) **Horizontal filing.** Containers are piled on top of each other in cabinets or drawers. This method should not be used if the papers are frequently referred to because of the difficulty in extracting files.
d. **Vertical filing.** Folders are placed behind each other in drawers. It facilitates easy withdrawal and insertion.
e) **Lateral filing.** Folders hang in open-fronted cabinets. Because of the absence of drawers there is a saving of floor space of the absence of drawers there is a saving of floor space and the cabinets can be higher than in vertical filing.

13. *Internal audit*

This operates in a similar way to the practice of professional auditors but it is done by specialists within the staff. It is usually a continuous process but it should not accord to a pattern. Thus, cashiers should not know when an auditor is expected nor should they be warned of a visit. Any audit involving cash must be carried out in the presence of the person responsible so that he can he can confirm the auditor's count.

The term can also include a special check on the books of a suspected member whilst he is away from the office.

14. *Internal check*

This implies the planning of work so that as far as possible one person or group automatically as part their normal duties, checks the work of another. The possibility of fraud can be reduced by periodically changing the duties of the staff.

15. The Use of Forms

Where information has to be provided regularly and to a standard pattern, the obvious method of reporting is by the use of forms. The form will be designed to give the information required and will therefore be planned according to the demands of the person requiring that information. The objective is to ask questions which must be answered. The answers must be capable of being expressed concisely.

16. Design of Forms

The following rules apply in designing a form:

a) It must have a cleared illustrative title and a reference code
b) The questions asked must be directly answerable from available sources. Thus, any figure to be inserted must appear in the data held by the person completing the form.
c) The items should be numbered for ease of reference.
d) If the form is to be completed by typing, the line-spacing must accord with typewriter spacing must accord with typewriter spacing.
e) If it is to be completed in handwriting the paper must be of a suitable quality.
f) The answer areas must be adequate to contain the required information.
g) The quality of the paper must take account of the amount of handling anticipated.
h) Filing must be considered. The forms must be of a standard size; margins must be wide if the forms are to be spine-bound or punched.
i) Distinctive colours should be used if the form is to have copies.
j) Appearance is important. The items must be neatly arranged and the typeface uniform.

17. The Use of Forms

The information provided by completed forms must be capable of easy extraction. In most cases, a number of similar types of returns will be received from various sources and it is therefore necessary to be able to easily compile a master return from the individual forms. Such an operation lends itself to mechanisation and it is useful for statistical purposes. Because all the forms of the same type ask the same questions it is possible to make comparisons between returns from different sources and between different periods.

18. Forms Control

Forms must be constantly reviewed. By so doing it is possible to amend a form if it no longer provides all the information required or if it gives information no longer needed. On occasions it may be found that a form is not longer required at all, either because the information is now irrelevant or because it is available from another form.

REFERENCE

- Shafritz, J.M. et al—"Introducing Public Administration" (2009)
- Jim Collins—"Good to Great" (2001)
- Peter Koestenbaum—Leadership: The Inner Side of Greatness (2006)
- The Institute of Administrative Management, England website
- The Essentials of Marketing—Research & Education Association, USA
- Wikipedia, the free encyclopedia
- The Association of Business Executive, England website
- Fortune Financial & Business Magazine

ABOUT THE AUTHOR

DR. AMBROSE E. Edebe, served as the general secretary of the Morning Star Church, London, England, from 1985 to 1995. From 1992 to 1995, he also served as an administrative officer with the UK Department of Education in London, England. In 1990, he was awarded the Fellowship of the College of Teachers, England, for a research thesis in education.

After relocating to the United States in 1995, Dr. Edebe served at the Baltimore City Department of Social Services and retired as the district manager of the department in 2009. He currently serves as the president of Trinity Professional Services, LLC in Maryland, USA. In 1996, he was commissioned as a notary public by the governor of Maryland.

Dr. Edebe has earned various academic and professional qualifications, including a BS in business administration, a BS in general business, an MA in leadership and management, an MBA in business administration, a doctorate in ministry, and a PhD in theological studies. He has received various citations and awards, from the governor of Maryland, the Senate of Maryland, the mayor of Baltimore, the Baltimore County executive, and the Maryland Department of Human Resources. He is a member of Delta Mu Delta Honor Society in Business Administration, and Phi Beta Delta Honor Society for International Scholars. He is the author of the bestselling book: Your Women Did Prophesy.

He is a dynamic teacher and a regular speaker in national and international conferences. He is married to Josephine; and they are blessed with four children: Sarah, Mary, Elizabeth, and Samuel.